THIS BOOK
BELONGS TO

....
....

Table of Contents

Introduction	5
Chapter 1: An Overview of the Problem, a Solution, and a Game Plan	7
The Problem	7
The Solution	8
Four Key Elements in the Solution	8
Concerns about the Solution	13
Acquiring the Skill Set to End the Cycle	14
A Game Plan to Achieve the Solution	15
This Book Is about Center B Properties	23
Chapter 9: Development or Rehabilitation (Build to a 12 Percent Yield)	25
The 10 Phases of a Construction or Rehab Project	25
Assessing a Construction Project	26
Developer as Conductor	28
Does the Project Hit Your Minimum Yield?	30
Argus Developer	33
Feasibility or Market Study	39
The Composition of a Feasibility Study	40
Residual Land Value	40
Preleasing	42
Equity and Financing	42
Mechanics' Liens	43
Liability under the Construction Loan	44
Design and Construction Drawings	44
Governmental Approvals	45
Covenants, Conditions, and Restrictions (CC&Rs)	47
Ground Lease Restrictions	47
Construction of Improvements in a Ground-Up Development	48
Inspections	50
Insurance	51
Decisions, Decisions, Decisions	52
Communication, Communication, Communication	53
Graphic Time Line	54

    Project Operating Costs   58

    Lender's Disbursement Form   59

    Change Orders   65

    Rehabilitation Project   65

    Construction of Improvements in a Rehab Project: Decisions, Decisions, Decisions   68

    Rehab Project: Communication, Communication, Communication   68

    Summary   69

Chapter 10: Marketing, Leasing, and Management   70

    Definition of Marketing, Leasing, and Management   70

    Marketing   71

    Leasing   77

    Strategy   77

    Management   108

    Management as a Business   118

    Conclusion   119

List of Abbreviations

Act	The Securities Act of 1933
Cap X	Capital Expenditures
CFBT	Cash Flow before Taxes
Code	Internal Revenue Code
DCR	Debt Coverage Ratio
FMV	Fair Market Value
IRR	Internal Rate of Return
LLC	Limited Liability Company
LP	Limited Partnership
LTV	Loan to Value
NOI	Net Operating Income
NPV	Net Present Value
NRSF	Net Rentable Square Foot
PSA	Purchase and Sale Agreement
PSF	Per Square Foot
PV	Present Value
ROA	Return on Assets
ROE	Return on Equity
SEC	Securities and Exchange Commission
1031	Section 1031 of the Internal Revenue Code

Introduction

This book is the result of many people asking me "How can I buy income-producing property? How can I get into the game?" The underlying purpose in this book is to set forth a practical step-by-step process on how to acquire commercial real estate and through a real estate vehicle build significant wealth over time. The discussion runs from sourcing a real estate transaction to analyzing the deal to acquiring the sticks and stones to managing real property to improving its value and finally to taking steps to preserve the value created and hopefully passing a good part of it on to your children and your children's children.

Unfortunately, there is a wealth of books on real estate that in essence say, "You can't lose. Go out and buy real estate!" You can lose in real estate just as in any other business. I usually buy from someone who has "lost"; that is, the value of the property and their equity therein has decreased from the date of their purchase. It is therefore essential to understand the fundamentals of the real estate game, including how to evaluate a real estate transaction and how to create value before you take the plunge and start to buy.

The text is geared to the novice who wants to understand commercial real estate as well as the seasoned professional who desires to enhance his knowledge. One of the key teaching tools revolves around setting forth a hypothetical that starts with the basics and then continually builds on the fact pattern to demonstrate real estate principles and theory and enhance the project analysis.

Although the concepts herein can be applied to all types of real estate, the focus is directed toward a project size of 30,000 to 150,000 square feet as is typically found in a neighborhood shopping center rather than a huge office building or a complex of over 500,000 square feet that might be found in a downtown high rise tower or a regional shopping mall.

Many individuals in the real estate field specialize in one area and therefore have a difficult time understanding and learning practical knowledge about other areas of real estate ownership. This text attempts, to some extent, to fill this gap. By covering a broad range of real estate topics from basic terminology and analysis to leasing, financing, marketing, management, structuring a partnership, real estate tax consequences, buying and selling real property, and the steps to take to preserve wealth, hopefully the reader can focus on the areas of his or her deficiencies.

Although I am an attorney by background, *This Book* is not intended as a legal treatise; rather, its focus is directed to the practical, day-to-day business aspects of acquiring, owning, and managing commercial real estate. I strongly recommend consulting with an attorney, accountant, and other professionals when entering into a lease, a purchase and sale agreement, or when any technical issues arise.

CHAPTER 1

An Overview of the Problem, a Solution, and a Game Plan

The Problem

If you are like 99 percent of the people on this planet, you have a problem: Namely, you must work to make money to eat and live.

It is a vicious cycle. You get up at 7:00 a.m., get out the door by 8:00 a.m., arrive at work at 9:00 a.m., push paper around all day, and leave at 5:00 or 6:00 p.m. You follow the same routine day after day. Your net pay is, say, $70,000 per year, you give 20 to 25 percent away to Uncle Sam, and your annual living expenses eat up the remaining money. The net result at the end of the year is no savings—zero, a goose egg, *nada*.

The next year you get a big promotion and an accompanying raise of 5 to 10 percent (if you are lucky). You have been waiting all year for this big raise. Your family has grown from husband and wife to husband, wife, and baby, and now you are expecting your second child. All year you have been putting off buying the new, latest and greatest big-screen television system and the much-needed trip to Hawaii, not to mention replacing that overused, tired Acura with a new Mercedes. What do you do to satisfy these pent-up demands? How do you satisfy these desires that have driven you for the past couple of years? The answer is that you move out of that cramped 1,500-to 2,000-square-foot apartment into a "decent" 3,000-to 4,000-square-foot home with a real backyard, you buy on credit the big screen "deal," you take the family on the long-delayed vacation to Hawaii, you lease a new car, and so on. The point is that you find a way to spend your increased wages and, with inflation, you are back in the same breakeven position you were in when you started a year ago, or even worse, since you have significantly increased your debt position.

We have identified The Problem, the cycle: You are working to meet the necessities of life including paying your silent partners (the state and federal governments), and you are consuming any remaining cash to satisfy pent-up demands for goods and services.

The Solution

The question becomes, how do you break this cycle? What is The Solution?

There is no single right answer to this question. There are several solutions to The Problem. The best solution I have found lies within the realm of real estate. You buy a *value-added property*, by which I mean a property that through your focused efforts can be improved and enhanced so it is worth significantly more after your efforts than when you acquired the asset. Your efforts usually revolve around increasing occupancy, but it can be a myriad of other tasks such as improving the overall appeal of the property through structural or cosmetic changes or changing the tenants by bringing in more viable businesses or more synergistic users, and so forth. Let's call your first acquisition "Property Number 1." You then:

- Acquire Property Number 1.
- Lease up or otherwise improve Property Number 1.
- Refinance Property Number 1, pulling out monies in excess of the existing debt at least equal to the original equity invested.
- Invest the refinance proceeds into another property (Property Number 2).
- Continue to manage Property Number 1, reaping the benefit of the positive cash flow and earning a management fee.
- Lease up or otherwise improve Property Number 2.
- Refinance Property Number 2, pulling out monies in excess of the existing debt at least equal to the original equity invested.
- Invest the refinance proceeds into another property (Property Number 3).
- Continue to manage Properties Number 1 and Number 2, reaping the benefit of their positive cash flow and earning a management fee.
- Lease up or otherwise improve Property Number 3, and so forth.

Four Key Elements in the Solution

Why does this Solution break the cycle? Because of four key elements.

Key Element Number 1

First, you are no longer limited in your earning potential by your salary or by your professional endeavors; rather, you have become an investor. You have converted active income into passive income. When you sleep at night, when you go on a vacation, you continue to make money. Your assets appreciate (hopefully) in value over time and in the normal course of events each month you build equity by paying down the principal on your mortgage. A mortgage usually contains an amortization feature; therefore a portion of each payment reduces the outstanding loan balance and consequently increases your equity, everything else being unchanged.

Usually the individual caught in the cycle is employed, earning a good living, but his livelihood is based upon his own individual capacity to do a job and get paid for that work. The basis of The Solution is a move to a business model that has the capacity to create wealth, not only from individual effort, but also based upon market forces. If you correctly analyze the market and correctly perceive that *capitalization rates* or *cap rates* (the rate of return an investor requires to induce him to purchase a property for all cash without regard to financing) will likely fall from 10 percent to 7 percent, then, even if no other change occurs in the real property investment, your property value will increase significantly. Market forces have resulted in a value shift. Similarly, if you purchase a property in a growth community and the resulting population growth fuels an increased demand for goods and services, that results in an upward push in rents, which translates into a higher net operating income, and therefore an increased property value. Again, market forces have driven value upward.

It is important to understand the difference between *active income* and *passive income*.

Active income is income earned through services rendered or goods sold. What is meant by "services rendered"? The concept of services for hire includes the broad area that comprises everything from practicing medicine to providing janitorial services. "Goods sold" refers to any product sold, from real estate to pencils.

The more difficult and more esoteric question is: What is *passive income*? Simply put, what I mean by passive income is income earned *not* by rendering services or selling goods. This does not mean that you do not have to work to make passive income, but rather that your work is of a different nature. Owning stock in a company, or for that matter owning the company itself, is an example of creating passive income. The employees of the company perform the functions that generate profits and dividends for its shareholders. The point is that the owner of the stock did not actually have to perform "labor" to receive the dividends paid. Similarly, the owner of real estate earns profits from rents, yet he does not actually provide services to the public or sell goods to the public. The delivery of services or the sale of goods is the function of his underlying tenants.

I want to emphasize once more that earning passive income does not mean that you do not have to work. The stockowner must spend time researching or hiring someone to research profitable stock selections and the monitoring thereof. Also, the real estate entrepreneur must operate his properties or employ a property manager. It can be demanding to invest in the stock market or to own and manage real estate. The individual who establishes a profitable stock portfolio did his research or had research done on his behalf. He verified that the company whose stock was purchased has a good management team, reasonable liquidity to survive tough times, growing sales, and net profits. He might also have an insight into the industry trends relating to the applicable field. Similarly, owning and managing real estate is a business. It requires insight to know when to buy and when to sell, as well as where to buy and where not to buy. Once a property is acquired, someone must invoice the tenants, collect the rents, coordinate vendors, and deliver services to tenants to ensure efficient operation of the asset. Someone must lease-up vacant space and make strategic decisions ranging from tenant mix to the overall look of the property to whether or not to expand the project by building-out additional leasable square footage to whether to refinance or sell. If a decision is made to refinance or sell, an individual must decide under what terms to borrow or under what terms to sell.

Notwithstanding the above, being a stock investor or a real estate owner is, in general, more akin to managing an investment as opposed to running an operating business that might require hundreds of employees. Yes, to be successful you need insight into what to buy, but you can to a large extent outsource the selection of the asset, as well as its care and feeding thereafter. That said, a good full-time investor will, at a minimum, manage his managers, and a superior full-time investor will take an active role in his business even though his business is not, in general, a labor-intensive one.

Rule Number 1

Convert active income into passive income.

Key Element Number 2

The second crucial step in breaking the cycle is to create a cash-flow model that generates consistent monthly dollars that can be built upon so that within a certain time frame the monthly cash flow equals $2X.

In other words, relating this step back to The Solution, if, for example, Property Number 1 generates $10,000 per month in revenue, then acquiring and leasing-up Property Number 2, which generates $10,000 per month in revenue, results in a cumulative cash flow of $20,000 per month. Acquiring and working Property Number 3 results in another $10,000 per month in net cash flow for a cumulative $30,000 per month.

Obviously, stating the objective is quite a lot easier than locating a property and executing a game plan that will generate a significant positive cash flow. However, the important point is that, yes, it is important to build value, but it is also important to build monthly cash flow.

Rule Number 2
Create a monthly cash flow model and build upon that model.

Key Element Number 3

The third key element in breaking the cycle is knowing that size matters. It is simple math. If your profit is $50,000 per year on Property Number 1 and Property Number 2 is 10 times as large as Property Number 1 then, everything else being equal, Property Number 2 will generate $500,000 in profits per year! The potential profit is ten times that of the smaller project, but usually not ten times the amount of work.

I have also found that there is more "wiggle room" in larger transactions. When you are working with a small real-estate project, the potential options to make money typically are not as readily available when compared to a much larger investment. For example, in a large real property project there might be excess land, which might allow you to build additional improvements or increase the size of the existing structures. Parking and its relationship to the net rentable square feet of the project is crucial when analyzing the allowable square-foot size of a development. The parking requirements for medical office projects typically require five parking spaces for each one thousand square feet of office space. Consequently, if you have a 60,000-square-foot medical office building the required parking would be 300 spaces, that is, 60,000 divided by 1,000 equals 60 times 5 equals 300 spaces. If you in fact have 400 parking spaces, 100 "excess" spaces, you have ample parking to support an additional 20,000 square feet of improvements without having to add more parking. Assuming a parking ratio of five spaces per thousand square feet, the calculation is reflected in the following formula:

$$\frac{X(5)}{1,000} = 100 \text{ spaces}$$

"X" represents the amount of additional square footage you can build. To solve for "X" you would divide by 5 and multiply by 1,000.

$$\frac{X(5)1,000}{(5)1,000} = \frac{100(1,000)}{5}$$
$$X = 20(1,000) = 20,000$$

In a recent project in which I was involved, I had excess parking and so was able to expand the project size by enclosing balconies. On other projects the excess parking allowed me to build an additional structure on the medical building campus and, in the case of a retail development, on an "out-pad" (a parcel removed from the in-line retail shops). Alternatively, you could possibly lease any extra parking spaces to an outside user, such as a local restaurant or a car dealer.

Rule Number 3

Size matters. If possible, work on large projects.

Key Element Number 4

Lastly, in our capitalist society the trick is to be able to expand your real estate portfolio so that you can create an infrastructure that allows you to employ individuals still trapped in the cycle. Going back to the model, The Solution builds in growth. You buy Property Number 1, lease it up or otherwise create value, refinance it, buy Property Number 2, continue to manage Property Number 1, reaping the benefits of the positive cash flow and the management fee, lease up or otherwise create value in Property Number 2, refinance it, buy Property Number 3, continue to manage Properties Number 1 and Number 2, reaping the benefits of their positive cash flow and management fees, and so on.

Growth is implicit in the model. You acquire additional properties and manage the new properties acquired as well as the previously acquired properties. It is therefore important to hire personnel who can competently run the properties once you acquire them. Delegation is crucial. How can you search for Property Number 4 if you have to focus all of your energy on managing Properties 1, 2, and 3?

In the long run, my philosophy and opinion is that in order to keep valuable employees/partners you must involve them in the business so that they have the opportunity to participate in the company's growth and success and thereby also break out of the cycle.

> ### Rule Number 4
> Create an economic environment that allows your employees, your team, to become invested in the future success of your company and allows them the means to be able to eventually break out of the cycle.

Concerns about the Solution

Keep in mind that no solution is a panacea. If you find yourself at a cocktail party and hear someone saying, "Buy real estate, you can't lose!" know that they are not telling the whole story, or that they have had one too many martinis. *Caveat emptor*. Care must be taken when purchasing real property. Buying real estate does not guarantee a profit. You can also lose money! If you purchase properties that have problems or that develop issues, your result may be a negative cash flow. Real property value is based upon rents derived from the project. If major tenants do not renew their leases or if they breach their leases and vacate the property, the resulting cash-flow disruption usually translates into problems. You can end up feeding the property instead of reaping a positive cash flow. What is more, purchasing marginal properties with marginal returns does not result in wealth creation. It results in marginal returns or even in losses if something goes wrong, which it often does. In part, proper due diligence procedures and follow-up on your part will avoid these results, but ultimately it is your execution of a viable game plan and your vision and foresight that will make the difference between winning or losing.

There is also the question of how to get started. When discussing The Solution with individuals seeking to escape the earn-pay tax-spend cycle, the first and foremost comment I often hear is: "I can't achieve this. I can't afford the down payment to buy this." I believe a lack of capital can be overcome. However, I want to make it clear that I am not an advocate of the "nothing down" purchase. First of all, usually there is something wrong with these types of transactions: too much unperceived risk, undisclosed problems, and so forth. Second, even if this can be accomplished, it places too much burden on cash flow and greatly increases your risk of default.

The way to overcome a lack of capital is through firsthand knowledge and experience. The individual who applies himself through study and through practical work experience in the real estate field should be able to partner with a capital source. In order to be successful in this approach you should, ideally, move beyond obtaining your college degree in real estate, beyond securing your real estate license, and beyond accumulating professional experience in a real estate field such as real estate investment sales, financing, or appraisals. What is most useful is to specialize in a specific product type in a specific local geographic area or areas. By focusing on a specific product in a specific area, you gain the market knowledge you need to be able to identify undervalued projects as well as to develop a strategy whereby you may execute and create value through management skills and contacts you have nurtured. The key is to gain the know-how and the knowledge to understand whether one transaction or another will result in a superior return and to know how to move an investment from a marginally performing property to a phenomenally performing asset.

Acquiring the Skill Set to End the Cycle

Ideally, in order to break out of the cycle, you should focus on five areas. First, you need a basic understanding of accounting. Accounting is the language of business. This is not to suggest that you have to become a CPA, but an understanding that goes beyond college courses, a practical understanding, is helpful. Second, it is necessary to have an understanding of legal principles. Contract real estate law is a recurring element in real estate transactions. A lease, which is a binding legal contract between the landlord and the tenant, governs the economics of a project. Third, it is crucial to have a practical knowledge of real estate financing, since financing is usually 50 to 80 percent of a real estate transaction. Next, it is essential to understand the basic concepts of the field on which you are focusing. In real estate, it is important to have a grasp of basic real estate principles, for example, knowing the difference between a fee simple estate and a leasehold estate. It is necessary to be able to answer relevant questions such as, *If the property to be purchased is a leasehold, what provisions must be in the lease to make it mortgageable?* Lastly, you must know how to structure a transaction. This knowledge usually comes from a number of sources: experience, discussions with senior people in the field who have put transactions together, and studying Chapter 11 in this text!

A Game Plan to Achieve the Solution

In subsequent chapters of this book, I discuss The Solution in greater depth, but at this point it is important to understand the basic principles underlying The Solution:

- Converting active income into passive income.
- Establishing a monthly cash flow model.
- Understanding that size matters.
- Understanding that an infrastructure, a team, should be created to capitalize on investment opportunities that arise.

I have identified The Problem and The Solution. The next logical question is: How do you achieve The Solution? I could discuss taking responsibility for one's actions, and having a positive attitude. I could offer case studies showing ordinary people accomplishing seemingly impossible tasks. These elements are important and discussing them can be motivational, but my approach is, I believe, less theoretical and "heady." It is more practical and down to earth.

The objective in the balance of this book is to create a framework to achieve The Solution.

I set forth an outline, which I call a business plan. I then identify concrete goals and actions items or "to dos" that, when fulfilled, will allow you, over time, to carry out your business plan. To some extent, your business plan and your goals may overlap and the goals may be incorporated into the business plan. The distinction is that although the business plan may, at times, be lofty, its goals and action items are always detailed and specific. I call this methodology of achieving The Solution "The Game Plan."

The Business Plan

One of the product types I have specialized in is medical office buildings. Part of my time is spent counseling my doctor tenants on how to run their businesses.

Medical schools do not, but should, teach doctors how to run a small business. To be successful, solo practitioners must understand where their lead sources come from and how to solicit these leads. They must also understand contracting, collections, personnel issues, and more. These subjects are not part of the medical school curriculum.

The first question I ask a doctor when I sit down with him or her is: Do you have a written business plan? Invariably the answer is "no." It is a mistake not to have a written business plan, especially for doctors who are just starting out in their practice. Established doctors usually have solidified their referral sources. Doctors that are just starting their practice usually have not created a solid referral base. By committing the business plan to writing it can be more systematically and logically analyzed and therefore improved upon, so a plan of action can be more effectively implemented.

My number one objective in a business plan is to bring out issues so they can be reflected upon and so that creative methods of dealing with these issues may be identified. I attempt to think outside the box.

There is no set format for a business plan. I prefer a written narrative business plan rather than bullet points. I find that a narrative generates thought and analysis rather than cursory conclusions. Suggested topics to cover in a business plan may be found in books devoted to this subject or even on the Internet. My narrative business plan attempts to cover the following nine areas.

1. A short summary of what the business is all about. What are you trying to accomplish? This section summarizes the entire plan. For example: *Purchase 50 million square feet of neighborhood shopping centers nationwide under centralized common ownership and management and then take the venture public by forming a real estate investment trust.*

2. A description of the business. Where is the business to be based? What product or service is to be provided? Who are the target customers? What price range is the focus?

3. The philosophical viewpoint of the business. The fundamental core values go beyond making money. Of course, the objective in a for-profit business is to make money, but this part of the plan should focus on ethics and assist in creating an ethical guide for the company.

4. An organizational guide. An organizational guide covers legal structure, percentage ownership, the composition of the management team including the function of each member, compensation, and an organizational chart indicating who reports to whom. In the context of a real estate company, the structure of the property management team should be addressed and possible anticipated staffing needs might be covered.

5. Product or service? This section contains a detailed description of the product or service to be delivered. Again, in the real estate context, such issues as the company's acquisition criteria including size, location, product type, number of tenants, vacancy factor, capitalization rate, internal rate of return over a 10-year period, and so forth, may be covered. Part of the plan should also cover existing owned product—for example, steps needed to enhance existing owned shopping centers might be covered.

6. Marketing. In the real estate context, this section should cover both the acquisition of new product as well as the lease-up of existing owned projects. Should your acquisition efforts be geared to working with brokers, direct advertisements, cold calls, or a combination of these methods? Should filling vacant space be done through working with outside brokers, internal staff, or a combination of these two approaches? Extensive thought and effort should be placed in this section since marketing is pivotal between sterling success and mediocre results. (Please refer to Chapter 10 for additional comments regarding designing a marketing program for the lease-up of a project.)

7. Financial analysis. How is the company doing overall? What does the income and expenses of each project look like? Annual budgets should be generated for each project with comparison columns to last year's results. This section might also cover funding needs for the company as well as possible sources of capital.

8. Future strategies. Strategies for expansion and issues surrounding growth might be covered in this portion of the business plan.

9. Miscellaneous. This is a general catch-all category of broad and specific company issues and matters not specifically covered above, such as ways to improve employee and organizational performance.

Goals

Regarding goals, I set annual goals and long-term goals, that is, things I want to accomplish within the year and objectives for five-plus years out. My personal system is to write up my goals mid-year in June or July and then revise, update, and finalize my goals late December through New Year's Day.

I feel it is important not to have a thousand goals. It is my belief that if you have too many goals, your energy is dissipated and you accomplish nothing. I attempt to limit my goals to 10, with an absolute maximum of 12.

After I have written and revised my goals I post them at my bedside. I read them when I go to bed at night and again when I wake up in the morning. Consequently, they are constantly in my mind's eye. If you desire to accomplish something, focusing unwaveringly on that task is the best way to achieve the desired result. If you wish to own and operate your own trash removal business, if you get up each day and labor hard, working the same route, picking up the trash and driving the truck to the dump, thinking *how quickly can I get this over with?* you will never reach your objective. However, by contrast, if you get up each day saying *I want to own my own garbage disposal company* and follow the logical action items necessary to get there—namely, obtaining an understanding of how business works through college and practical work experiences and saving enough capital to buy your first truck—and if you couple this with working in the business from the trash pick-up end through the administrative end, the likelihood of reaching your goal becomes highly probable.

Action Items or "To Dos"

In addition to the overall business goals mentioned above, I also view each property as a business and therefore set forth specific goals for each property.

Once the business plan and goals are established, I list detailed action items to enable me to reach my goals. In my real estate business, I first list on a separate piece of paper every property I own. Under the various properties, I specify "To Dos."

I have found that there are matters that do not fit into specific property categories. Therefore, I create what I call Special Project Lists to catch the other areas outside specific property action items.

Gary's Lists

The projects "To Dos" are then prioritized into a First Priority List and a Second Priority List. The task is to rank, in order of importance, the tasks to be accomplished. My First Priority List consists of matters of utmost importance that should be focused on immediately and completed immediately. The Second Priority List is important, but not, obviously, as important as the First Priority List.

I keep the lists on my computer, which facilitates the updating process. My daily review of the priority lists is cursory, because I want to get going, accomplishing the tasks on the list.

I also write up a daily To Do list. The Daily List usually contains a few items from the First Priority List and a few items from the Second Priority List, as well as other things that can be accomplished relatively quickly. The Daily List consists of things that must be done that day, for example, returning specific telephone calls, as well as work that must be furthered that day, such as finalizing a lease or a Purchase and Sale Agreement. The Daily List is made of the crucial items on the Priority Lists plus items that can be addressed and disposed of quickly.

After I have created a Daily List, I select the most important items that must be focused on immediately. I refer to these items as my Short List. These are no more than five items that must be substantially completed by the next business day. I always work on these items first when I walk into the office.

The key for me is to review and update my lists for at least 30 to 60 minutes every weekend, usually Sunday night, and then take one item at a time, going down the list and getting one item completed so it can be removed from the List or at least put into play so that it can be worked on until accomplished.

Please refer to Exhibit 1.1 for a graphic illustration of The Game Plan. The Game Plan is organized from the bottom up. The business plan serves as the foundation, and then the goals are established. The "To Dos" build upon the goals, for it is through accomplishing the "To Dos" that the goals are achieved. Lastly the "To Dos" are pared down and prioritized until you come to the Priority Lists and the Daily List and Short List of super-important items that must be worked on immediately.

Rule Number 5

Think out and commit to paper what you wish to accomplish. Keep detailed lists of action items.

Exhibit 1.1 **The Game Plan**

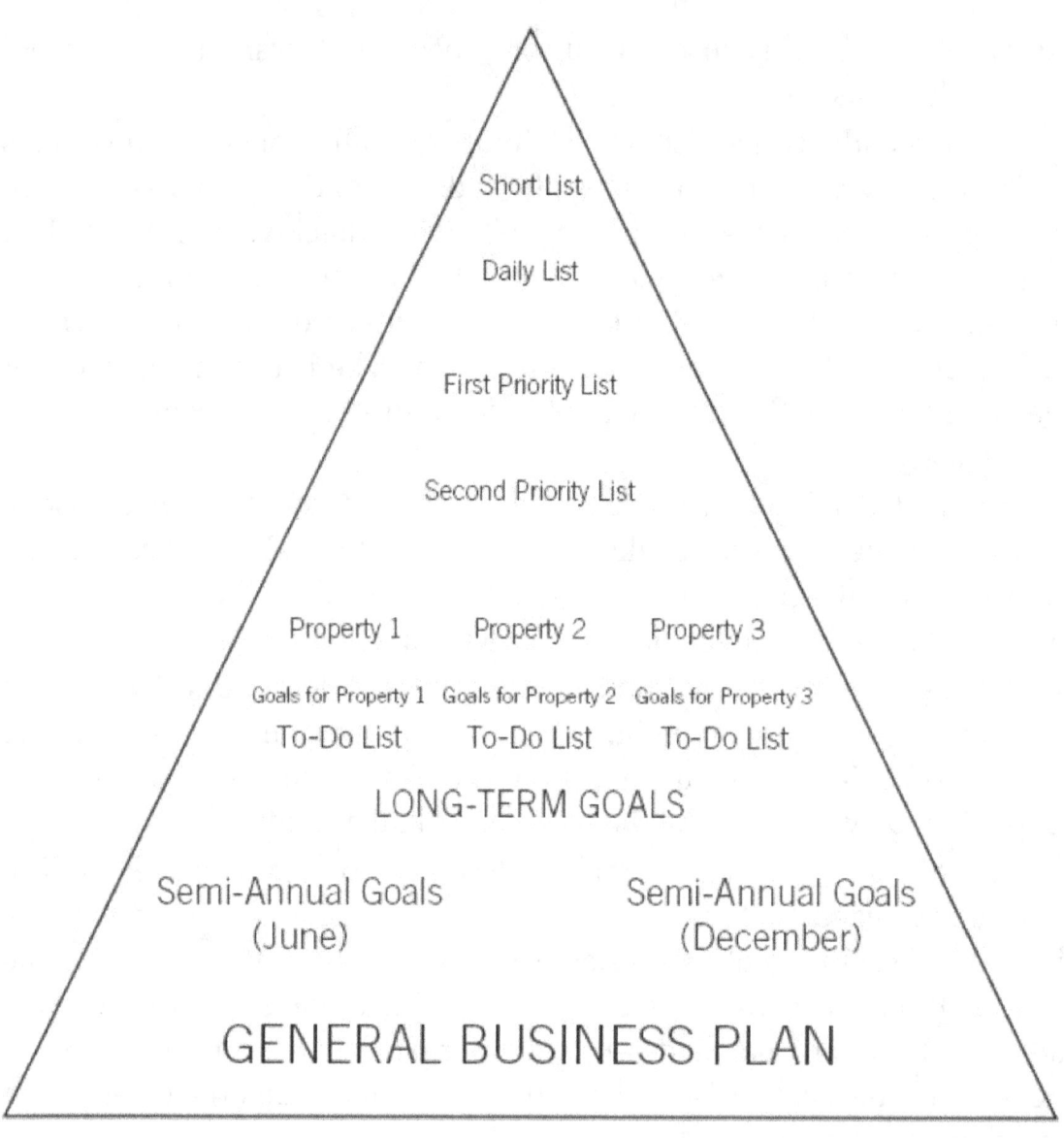

If you can envision how to get from point A to point Z, that is, from an underperforming property to a fully leased successful transaction, that is half of the battle. The other half, however, is execution: doing the tasks necessary to get there. Execution can encompass everything from negotiating and consummating leases to hiring excellent vendors to servicing your complex. Without execution, vision falls short. Following through on the "To Dos" translates into execution.

> # Rule Number 6
> Success equals vision with execution.

Focus, Focus, Focus

Another key to success, one that has more of an effect on success than education, capital, experience, desire, or personality type, is focus. Focus has two subcategories: concentration and discipline.

No Flip-Flopping

If you start out in business as a mortgage broker and then, after two years, decide you want to be a stock-broker, and then after two more years decide you want to sell insurance, your success ratio will probably not be very high. Hopscotching from one business to another results in failing to become an expert on anything. The consequence is that you never develop a clientele, never develop a network for referrals, vendors, and colleagues. You never develop a success formula if you keep switching from one field to another.

Stick with the Task at Hand

Develop discipline to concentrate on the task at hand no matter how unpleasant it might be or how much you would rather watch a television program or a movie, take a nap, or go for a walk in the park.

> ### Rule Number 7
> Focus on one field, no flip-flopping. Focus on one task at a time and get that task done before moving on to task number 2.

Please note that sticking with the task at hand does not mean devoting more time to it than it requires. I was recently having dinner with a couple and the wife bemoaned the fact that her husband worked so hard. She kept complaining that they had no family life because her husband constantly worked to pay the bills. It is not how many hours you put in that counts; it is results that matter. You measure achievement by results, not the length of time you work on a project. Often the more time and effort you put into a task translates into accomplishment, but not necessarily. If you get the job done and it takes one hour, isn't that more impressive than if you worked all night on the project? The "kill yourself" work ethic makes no sense. Results speak for themselves.

> ### Rule Number 8

> Judge yourself by your results, not by how long or hard you work.

Risk versus Reward

Every investor knows, or should know, that there are risks involved in a real estate investment. The general rule is that there is an inverse relationship between risk and reward: the greater the risk, the greater the return. Conversely, the rule states that the lower the risk, the lower the return. The trick is to identify the risks and then balance risk and reward by eliminating as much of the risk as possible while still achieving an acceptable return. Risk management is inherent in any investment, including a real estate project. The successful real estate entrepreneur focuses on the downside and structures the transaction to minimize the risk factors.

> ## Rule Number 9
> Look at the downside. Identify the risk areas in a project and put in place a strategy to cushion these risks, to the extent possible.

Identifying Opportunities

Assume there are two shopping centers in close proximity to each other. Both centers are about the same size, 150,000 net rentable square feet, and in comparable condition. Center A is 100 percent leased and occupied, while Center B is 50 percent leased and occupied. Center A is being offered for sale at $15,000,000 ($100 per square foot) while Center B is being sold for $7,500,000 ($50 per square foot). Which is the better buy? This is a trick question. There is no clear-cut answer. Most important, there is not sufficient information to make an informed decision. You do not know, among other things, the income and expenses of the centers. The underlying credit behind the rental income might be far stronger in one or the other center. You also do not know the maturity date of the existing leases or the rent escalation schedules or the tenants' payment history. Nor do you know how well the tenants are doing, what is happening in the local community that might affect each project, or the overall strength of the leasing market.

In general, however, your decision depends to a large extent on your financial goals and risk posture. If you manage a large pension fund, then Center A, if it meets your yield criteria, would probably be your selection. It is fully leased, so it probably generates a stable cash flow. By contrast, if you are entrepreneurial, Center B is probably your choice, given its upside potential. It is only 50 percent leased so as you lease additional space, value is created.

This Book Is about Center B Properties

The focus of this book is value-added properties: Identifying value-added real estate, discovering creative strategies to enhance the value of a project, and executing those strategies. Usually, everything else being equal, the property with vacant space will sell for a higher *cap rate* than the real estate that is fully leased. The seller will argue that, given the upside potential in Center B, the buyer should pay a higher price. In a 100-percent-leased center the only way to go is down, in other words, to lose occupancy.

Again, in this example, there is not enough information about the two centers to make an informed decision. Possibly Center A is also a value-added B type of property. For example, possibly the rents are significantly under market so as to afford a buyer the opportunity to work the center when leases turn to significantly increase cash flow. However, in general, it is Center B that has the clear potential to grow and increase its value through leasing the vacant space.

Typically, when a property comes on the market, multiple potential buyers view the offering. The successful real estate player analyzes the project, figures out a game plan to increase cash flow, and then, taking the cost of his strategy into account and factoring in an acceptable yield, makes an appropriate offer.

The strategy to enhance cash flow might involve altering the physical elements of the project. The alterations might be as simple as adding attractive new paint colors and fresh landscaping or as extensive as a full exterior stucco remodel, with a change in the project's physical orientation.

The success of a retail project is often heavily dependent on the availability of convenient and ample parking. Envision a major box tenant with limited parking on the north side of the building. The developer acquires an acre of land on the south side of the building and reorients the entrance so that customers enter the store from the south side where there is an abundance of paved parking. Similarly, envision a movie theater operator whose business has adequate parking, but the location of parking is undesirable, since it is subterranean and tandem in nature (i.e., cars are parked so that one car might block another car).

To enhance the desirability of his theater, the movie theater operator may enter into an agreement with the adjacent medical building owner so that his customers may use the extensive surface parking from the medical building lot after 5:00 p.m., when most doctors are no longer seeing patients.

A change in the nature of the tenants may dramatically affect the success of a center. A reorientation of tenants in a center from those that have nothing in common to those that have a synergistic relationship and can cross-refer clients may dramatically improve a property. Replacing weak mom-and-pop tenants with strong credit tenants might improve the financial performance of the project.

Change, whether it is a governmental rule and regulation change, or a change relating to the business climate in general, equals opportunity. The key is to be aware of the change and to take advantage of the opportunity that it offers. If you are considering building an assisted living facility and the state significantly increases the density requirements, altering your plans to take advantage of these developments might have a significant positive effect on profitability. Similarly, in a recessionary environment, players who are capital rich are usually able to take advantage of advantageous pricing. Should not purchases be made when values are depressed? Of course! Often, however, the difficulty is in determining when to buy. Will values continue to fall? Where is the bottom? This is where your knowledge, your research, and your strategizing come in. Remember, hearing opportunity knock is one thing; knowing when to open the door is another.

Rule Number 10

To effectively play the real estate game, it is crucial to identify opportunities and figure out strategies to take advantage of these opportunities.

CHAPTER 9

Development or Rehabilitation (Build to a 12 Percent Yield)

Getting involved with a construction project is usually more complex and time-consuming than the purchase of an existing real estate investment. If you are considering new construction or a major rehabilitation (rehab) project, there are many variables to consider.

The 10 Phases of a Construction or Rehab Project

A ground-up development or a major rehab project can be broken down into 10 distinct phases:

1. Equity assemblage
2. Feasibility study
3. Acquisition of the land and/or the project
4. Acquisition and development financing
5. Design and construction drawings
6. Governmental approvals
7. Construction of improvements
8. Marketing and leasing
9. Permanent loan
10. Management and operation of the project

A straight acquisition of a leased fee estate usually does *not* include four of these phases: the feasibility study, design and construction drawings, governmental approvals, and, of course, the construction phase. These four areas are discussed in this chapter, along with other construction-related matters. The other areas are covered in more depth in other chapters.

The 10 phases just listed are often interdependent and do not necessarily follow in a consistent, linear order. It makes sense to obtain your equity monies at the outset, but there is nothing wrong with seeding the project with your own funds and later, if you decide to move forward, assembling all of the needed capital. Similarly, in order to complete the feasibility study, it is crucial to understand the applicable construction costs, which are dependent on the design and the final construction drawings. A permanent loan is typically secured only once the project is fully built and substantially leased with tenants in place; however, it might be desirable or necessary to obtain a take-out commitment (a lender agrees to fund a specified dollar amount at a later date subject to certain conditions being fulfilled) prior to starting the project. The construction lender, for example, might require a take-out commitment as a condition of its construction loan. In addition, on income-producing projects, such as retail, office, or industrial construction, a preleasing level is often part of a construction lender's requirements. If preleasing is required, marketing and leasing predates all of the other phases. Governmental approvals, such as permits, are usually obtained after the construction documents are submitted to the building and safety department, although typically the developer has had multiple discussions with the city planning department or other governmental agencies well in advance of the formal submission. The point is that the phases interact and overlap. The foregoing are merely examples of the interrelationship of the various phases.

Assessing a Construction Project

Imagine you are driving in your car and you see a large vacant lot near a hospital with a huge sign on the property captioned "Land for Sale—Can Build 60,000 Square Foot Medical Office Building." The sign also has a broker's name and phone number.

How do you determine whether or not a project makes sense on this piece of dirt? What are the criteria for judging if a development project is viable? The sign suggested building a medical office building. The land is located in close proximity to a hospital. However, the question still remains: Is a medical office building the highest and best use for this property? Would it be better to build medical condominiums or a mixed-use project with retail in the area fronting the street, reserving the balance of the development for medical office space? What if there is already a medical office building on the hospital's campus that is almost entirely vacant, but the hospital employees are having a difficult time finding affordable living space? Would an apartment building make more sense? If you decide you would like to move forward and build a project, what should you pay for the land?

The first step is to collect additional information about the project. You call the broker listed on the "for sale" sign and ask general questions. Is the property still for sale and, if so, what is the asking price? How long has the lot been for sale? What is the profile of the seller? What is the seller's motivation for selling? Would the seller consider a joint venture? What is the lot size? What is the zoning? Is there any preleasing? Have there been any potential leasing inquiries? Where are the potential tenant-demand generators? Is there an architect involved and, if so, has he completed a preliminary site plan and/or construction drawings? Are there any potential problems with the site such as compacted land, drainage issues, or environmental problems? These questions are merely a starting point in the inquiry stage. There are many additional questions to raise and to which you must determine the answers. A potential buyer should, however, consider that, from a negotiation standpoint, it is important to show restraint in the amount and number of questions asked at the initial contact stage. It is important to establish a rapport with the seller and/or the seller's agent at this juncture. Making further inquiries as you go along, as well as retaining the proper experts to help you gather information, will hopefully clear up many of the unknowns. Let us assume that after a preliminary inquiry you decide to learn more about the project. You hire an engineer—and perhaps an architect—who reviews zoning and determines the type of construction that is permissible and the potential density of your project, given the site constraints. Usage will dictate parking requirements, which are often the constraining factor when ultimately configuring the size of the structure that can be built.

You might hold a meeting with the appropriate city planning official, with your engineer or architect in attendance, to better understand what the property is entitled for, that is, exactly what may be built on the site at this time. What does the City or the appropriate governmental entity want on this site? Additional questions might include: What are the set back restrictions? Are there any special assessments? Are utilities, for example, gas, water, electric, brought to the site? How far away is the hook-up to the city sewer system? Does the city have any special rules, such as unusual drainage requirements?

If you elect to go further with the project the site should be placed under contract, since money must be spent on due diligence items at this point, if not earlier. Ideally, from the buyer's perspective, the purchase and sale agreement

(PSA) should allow the buyer an adequate period of time to conduct due diligence without risking capital with the seller. Enough money must be spent on due diligence at the initial stages of the project without additional nonrefundable funds being paid to the seller. Usually, at this stage, the seller will permit a buyer to tie up the property to conduct studies to determine if the site works for him. The issue becomes one of timing. What is a reasonable time to hold the property under a contract to purchase without a firm commitment from the buyer? From a developer's point of view, the ideal scenario is to tie up the dirt without committing nonrefundable monies until he is ready to put a spade in the ground. From the seller's perspective, a reasonable period should be given the buyer during which he may explore the viability of the project and the site—but then the buyer must commit so the refundable good faith deposit becomes a nonrefundable deposit, applied to the purchase price if the buyer closes, yet retained if the buyer fails to close. A compromise position might be for the seller to give the buyer a few months to explore the viability of the project and then, if the buyer desires additional time, for the seller to stipulate that the good faith deposit becomes nonrefundable and increases in size as additional time to close is given.

Developer as Conductor

In a construction project, the developer/owner becomes the conductor, orchestrating and managing the various parties who contribute their work to the project in an attempt to create a final product. The orchestra must be assembled. An architect is needed to analyze the site to determine the size of the project that can be placed on the land as well as its configuration. The architect might consult with a civil engineer who focuses on grading, streets, and sewers, and overall utility systems. Later in the process the architect may consult with other engineers, such as a mechanical engineer, who designs the building's HVAC system, and an electrical engineer, who is usually retained to design the electrical power and distribution system. An attorney is needed to assist in, among other things, drafting the PSA, reviewing the survey in conjunction with the preliminary title report. Additional expertise might be needed in the following areas: an appraiser, an environmental assessment company, a soils engineer, a title company, a surveyor, a landscape architect, a bonding company, a leasing broker, a mortgage broker and/or a lender, a space planner, an interior designer, parking consultants, an artist who creates "public art," a public relations and/or an advertising agency, a property management company, and a contractor who oversees various subcontractors or other tradesmen. The long list of potential subcontractors to be hired by the contractor might include a grading contractor, a foundation expert, an electrician, a plumber, HVAC professionals, a flooring company, individuals to do demolition or framing, tile installers, insulation experts, painters, drywall installers, stucco/plastering specialists, sprinkler companies, elevator firms, lighting consultants, and the like.

The developer is ultimately responsible for overseeing the various parties in the orchestra. If something goes wrong, it is usually the owner who will bear the brunt of the problem in terms of time and money. It is therefore crucial for the developer to strike a balance between selecting expert, skilled members of the team, at an affordable price, and personally supervising the contracted parties. The developer cannot be everywhere. He cannot oversee all steps in the process, but, obviously, he should not close his eyes. He must monitor, at least on a spot basis, the construction flow and the activities of key project members. It is because of this reasoning that, especially on larger project, the developer often has a full-time construction manager onsite who is an employee of the developer and whose function it is to monitor and coordinate the project.

A soils report will answer questions about the condition of the soil, for example, whether or not there is any landfill, whether toxic materials are present, and whether the soil has the ability to support the planned structure. The architect, in consultation with an engineer, can draft a site plan for the project and lay out a building footprint and foundation. A preliminary title report and a survey are needed to set the site boundaries as well as locate easements and any potential encroachments. It is important to locate any underground utility lines or other cabling. If the grading company hits an unidentified large fiber-optic line, the necessary repairs can be costly. If the land is not on a level surface, the survey might include a topographic map showing elevations that may have a bearing on the ability to develop the site and on density issues.

In addition to working with advisors, the developer must also interface with various levels of the city government including the planning staff, building and safety, inspectors, and possibly the city council. Development can be controversial. The size, design, and scope of a project, along with its resulting traffic patterns and parking requirements, may result in neighborhood or homeowner associations having concerns that must be addressed.

Does the Project Hit Your Minimum Yield?

Let us say you learn that the project is zoned commercial, that it includes a medical office, that it comprises 132,605 square feet (3.047 acres), and that the asking price is $663,050 ($5.00 per square foot). How do you determine whether or not this project makes economic sense?

Referring back to the chapter's subtitle, what is meant by "Build to a 12 Percent Yield?" Put simply, you have to determine what minimum percentage yield or return is necessary to induce you and your investors to invest in the project. Factors such as area demographics, potential project size, preleasing levels and absorption assumptions, community acceptance or resistance, the structure of the financing, or the tenant mix and quality may be decisive factors in your decision to move forward or to back away. Yet, typically, the initial screening test revolves around the numbers: Does this potential project meet your yield requirements?

If we know the yield that we need to achieve is 12 percent and if we can also figure out the cost of building the project, the unknown, therefore, is the net income. What rental rate must be achieved to yield this return on a given cost? The formula we are working with is:

$$\frac{\text{Net Income}}{\text{Project Cost}} = \text{Yield} = \text{Return on Cost}$$

We therefore might build an economic model with the unknown being the rent you are going to charge tenants. We might work backwards, first estimating the total project cost. To simplify the analysis, we are going to assume that the building will be preleased to a single tenant and that it will take one year to build the building and get the tenant in place paying rent.

For the proposed 60,000-square-foot medical office building, the construction costs might be estimated as follows:

Hard Costs	
Improvements 60,000 @ $100 per sq. ft. plus One Elevator	$6,000,000
On/Off Site Improvements 81,000 sq. ft. @ $12 per sq. ft.	972,000
Tenant Improvements 56,000 sq. ft. @ $50 per sq. ft.	2,800,000
Hard Cost Contingency	600,000
Land Cost	
3.047 acres @ $5.00 per sq. ft.	663,050
Soft Costs	
Architectural and Engineering	113,000
Plans/Permits	110,000
Interest Carry ($10,000,000 Loan 50% Disbursed for 12 Months at 7.5% Interest-Only)	375,000
Loan Fee (1%)	100,000
Legal	30,000

Legal	30,000
Title, Recording, and Escrow Expenses	27,000
Appraisal	5,000
Cost Analysis & Review	1,250
Inspections	6,000
Environmental and Review	2,000
Operating Expenses during Construction	40,000
Return to Investors during Construction	255,700
Soft Cost Contingency	400,000
TOTAL PROJECT COST	**$12,500,000**

In this analysis, we are assuming that no leasing commissions are incurred. This project is a build-to-suit. The assumption is that the developer has a longstanding relationship with the tenant and therefore does not go through a broker to locate the tenant or negotiate the lease. This, of course, might not be a valid assumption if the tenant has a contractual agreement with a broker and insists that that broker be paid regardless of the circumstances or, of course, if the project is to be multitenant (in which case at least a portion of the lease up will probably result in leasing commissions paid to outside real estate brokers). Also, the operating expenses during construction are fairly minimal since the downtime revolves around construction rather than lease-up. During the construction phase, taxes and insurance must be paid, but the operating expenses really kick in once the building is constructed. It is then that, in addition to taxes and insurance, other operating costs such as utilities and janitorial expenses are incurred. Furthermore, when calculating the overall project cost, a return to the capital partners is often overlooked. Most analyses do not factor in this cost, but if the project is syndicated it is a real expense. In our hypothetical scenario, the construction loan is assumed to be 80 percent of the construction costs, or $10,000,000. Therefore, the equity portion is 20 percent, or $2,500,000. At a 10 percent return to the investors, $250,000 in additional costs, as a preferred return, must be paid out to the money side of the investment during the year the project is under construction.

If you desire to achieve at least a 12 percent return on your investment, you must, on the average, charge rents of at least $2.23 per square foot per month on a triple net basis. The calculation is as follows:

> $12,500,000 total project costs times the target 12 percent return results in a required net operating income of $1,500,000 divided by the project total net rentable square footage of 56,000, equals an annual base rent of approximately $26.79 or on a monthly basis $2.23 net, net, net.

Relating this back to the chapter subtitle, "Build to a 12 Percent Yield" means, in this context, that the owner intends to construct the building so that after it is built and leased the yield on total cost will approximate a 12 percent return. The goal is to find a project that, based on reasonable assumptions, will be able to achieve the minimum acceptable yield. The 12 percent return on cost outlined above is based on the total estimated project cost.

In order to more fully evaluate the project, it is necessary to make assumptions as to projected income and expenses. Using the model developed for the Diamond Medical Center, which is a 60,000 medical office project, the income and expenses would look as follows:

Gross Income		**$1,440,000**
Expense Reimbursement		
Recapture over Base Year	18,000	
Utility Recapture	76,800	
Triple Net Charges	121,836	
Total Expense Reimbursement		216,636
Total Gross Income		$1,656,636
Vacancy and Collection Loss		(82,832)
Adjusted Gross Income		$1,573,804
Operating Expenses		
Elevator Contract	(11,197)	
HVAC Maintenance Contract and Repair	(5,413)	
Insurance	(5,000)	
Janitorial Contracts	(52,600)	
Landscaping	(6,410)	
Property Taxes	(97,067)	
Property Management Fee	(49,699)	
Repairs & Maintenance	(13,470)	
Security and Fire	(27,931)	
Taxes & Licenses	(420)	
Trash Disposal	(6,336)	
Utilities	(180,956)	
Total Operating Expenses		(456,499)
Net Operating Income		**$1,117,305**

Based on the foregoing, conclusions can be made as to the project's projected profitability, return on equity, and so on. For example, if we assume an 8 percent cap rate at sale, the net sales price, if we marketed the project after it was built and occupied, would be $13,547,323 ($1,117,305/.08 less a 3 percent sales commission). The result is an approximate $226 value per square foot ($13,547,323/60,000 square foot): Approximately a $1,000,000 profit on a $2,500,000 investment; and a 40 percent return on equity (ROE). This is a very respectable return, especially in light of the fact that we assumed that this project was a build-to-suit and, hence, the leasing risk was essentially eliminated.

However, please note that the projected NOI of $1,117,305 falls short of the required $1,500,000 needed to achieve the 12 percent yield on cost. The question then becomes, Is the yield sufficient to induce the developer and his investors to move forward with the project?

There must be a gap between the return on cost and NOI/Project Cost in order for there to be a profit. Here the return on cost is 12 percent and the NOI/Project Cost is assumed to be 8 percent. The result is a profit. If the return on cost is 8 percent, then by definition the NOI is $1,000,000 ($X$/$12,500,000 = .08, hence X equals $1,000,000). Unfortunately, under these assumptions, if the cap rate is also assumed to be 8 percent, then the fair market value is $12,500,000 ($1,000,000/.08). No profit would result.

From a cash flow perspective, if we assume a permanent loan replaces the construction loan for the same amount, $10,000,000, at the same interest rate, 7.5 percent interest only, again using our prior assumptions the cash flow would be as follows:

Net Operating Income	$1,117,305
First Trust Deed of $10,000,000 @ 7.5% I/O	(750,000)
Cap X Reserves	(18,000)
Tenant Improvements and Leasing Commissions	(60,000)
Net Cash Flow	$289,305

Based on a $2,500,000 cash investment, the annual leveraged return on equity (ROE) is 11.57 percent ($289,305/$2,500,000). (Please note: The acronym ROE is also often used interchangeably with the phrase "return on investment" [ROI]). Again, the issue becomes, Is this a sufficient return to motivate the builder and his capital sources to further explore the project?

Argus Developer

Argus has a specific program designed to assist a developer in analyzing a construction project. The program is called "Argus Developer."

Exhibit 9.1 contains an Excel "Project Pro Forma" that restates the project's projected income and expenses and development costs.

Exhibit 9.1 Argus Developer: Pro Forma

Project Pro Forma

REVENUE	%	$	$	$	$	$
Rental Area Summary	Units	ft²	Rate ft²	Unit Amount	Rent at Lease Start	Rent at Sale
Medical Offices	10	56,000	$2.14	$144,000	1,440,000	1,440,000
Investment Valuation						
Medical Offices – $82,832.00 non recov. cost						
Capitalized Rent	1,357,168	Cap Rate	8.00%	16,964,600		
Operating Expenses	–456,499	Cap Rate	8.00%	–5,706,238		
Tenant Reimbursements	216,636	Cap Rate	8.00%	2,707,950		
					13,966,312	
Sales Commission		3.00%	–508,938		–508,938	
Income from Tenants					1,357,168	
Additional Rent Revenue						
Tenant Reimbursements—Medical Offices					216,636	
Additional Rent Cost						
Operating Expenses—Medical Offices				–456,499		
Capital Reserves—Medical Offices				–18,000		
Tenant & LC—Medical Offices				–60,000		
					–534,499	
TOTAL PROJECT REVENUE						$14,496,679
DEVELOPMENT COSTS						

Project Pro Forma

REVENUE	%	$	$	$	$	$
Rental Area Summary	Units	ft²	Rate ft²	Unit Amount	Rent at Lease Start	Rent at Sale
ACQUISITION COSTS						
Land Cost	132,605 ft²	$5.00	663,025			
				663,025		
CONSTRUCTION COSTS						
Construction	ft²	Rate ft²	Cost			
Medical Offices	60,000	$100.00	6,000,000	6,000,000		
Contingency		10.00%	600,000			
Offsite Improvements	81,000 ft²	12 pf²	972,000			
				1,572,000		
TI Costs						
TI Cost Area Rate —Medical Offices		$50.00	2,800,000			
				2,800,000		
PROFESSIONAL FEES						
Architect & Engineering			113,000			
Plans/Permits			110,000			
Legal			57,000			
Appraisal			6,250			
Inspections			6,000			
Environmental Review			2,000			
Soft Cost Contingency			400,000			
Operating Expenses during Construction			40,000			
				734,250		
Total Costs before Interest and Fees						$11,769,275
Interest and Fees Included in Project Costs						
Interest Paid for Debt Sources: Construction Loan (7.50%)		267,006				
Total Interest Paid for Debt Sources:			267,006			

Project Pro Forma

REVENUE	%	$	$	$	$	$
Rental Area Summary	Units	ft²	Rate ft²	Unit Amount	Rent at Lease Start	Rent at Sale
Total Interest Included in Project Cost				267,006		
Fees Paid for All Sources: Construction Loan —Loan Fee (1.00%) (Single)			100,000			
Total Fees Paid for All Sources				100,000		
Total Interest and Fees Included in Project Costs				367,006		
Total Costs Including Funded Interest and Fees				12,136,281		
Interest and Fees not Included in Project Costs						
Mortgage Interest (7.50%)		746,874				
Total Interest Paid			746,874			
Debt Financing Fees Mortgage—% Fee (1.00%) (Single)			100,000			
Total Interest and Fees not Included in Project Costs				846,874		
TOTAL PROJECT COSTS						$12,983,155
PROFIT						$1,513,525
Performance Measures						
Profit on Cost%				11.66%		
Profit on GDV%				10.84%		
Development Yield% (on Rent)				15.03%		
Pre-Finance IRR%				15.03%		
Project IRR% (with Interest)				16.41%		
Equity IRR% (with Interest)				26.95%		
Return on Equity%				62.36%		

The vacancy and collection loss is referred to as "nonrecoverable costs." Used in connection with the inputted Excel figures is an Argus spreadsheet (see Appendix E on the companion website) outlining the income and expenses over a 31-month time frame. It is assumed it will take about six months to complete the plans and secure a permit, another year to build all of the offsite improvements, the medical office building, and the tenant improvements for the user, and another year to season and sell the project.

In the model, as is typically done, the preferred return to the investors is considered a distribution of profits shown when available rather than as a project cost. Assumptions are made in the spreadsheet as to when the construction funds are actually expended. For example, in month one, the land is purchased and hence $663,025 is disbursed. During the first six months of the development, plans and permits must be secured, and therefore monies are spent on soft costs such as architectural fees, appraisal costs, legal expenses, and so on. In month seven, actual construction activities commence and funds are expended for offsite improvements such as grading, curb cuts, sewer, and so forth, as well as the foundation for the building. The interest calculation in the previous section was calculated based upon an average outstanding balance. The Argus spreadsheet calculates the interest expense based on the assumed outstanding loan balance based upon the assumed disbursement schedule. A distinction is made in the pro forma between "Interest and Fees Included in Project Costs" and "Interest and Fees not Included in Project Costs." The distinction is based on timing. The included costs are assumed to be incurred during the build-out. The excluded costs relate to interest and fees on the permanent $10,000,000 loan originated after the construction is completed.

The Project Pro Forma then summarizes the project results under the heading "Performance Measures." The "Profit on Cost%" is equivalent to the previously discussed Yield. It is calculated as the profit of $1,513,525 divided by the Total Project Cost of $12,983,155. The Total Project Cost includes the interest and fees associated with the permanent financing. "Profit on GDV%" is the profit as a percentage of the Gross Development Value. This calculation equals the profit of $1,513,525 divided by the derived value. In the first part of the Excel pro forma, the "Investment Valuation" shows a $13,966,312 value based upon an 8 percent cap rate. The "Development Yield" is the project net cash flow including reductions for reserves of $1,039,305 over the Total Project Cost of $12,983.155. The "Return on Equity%" shows a healthy 62.36 percent. It is a function of the profit of $1,513,525 divided by the cash equity spent of $2,427,256. The cash equity could be a specified dollar amount or, as in this analysis, assumed to equal 20 percent of the Total Costs including Funded Interest and Fees. In other words, the equity is assumed to equal 20 percent of the Total Project Costs excluding costs associated with the permanent loan.

These ratios certainly give an indication of the project's health, but they are a snap shot in time. In contrast, the Internal Rate of Return (IRR) reflects a yield over the 31-month holding period. As discussed in Chapter 3, the internal rate of return is the discount rate when the present value of the project's cash flow equals the initial investment plus the present value of any additional capital contributions. In other words, the IRR is the discount rate when the net present value is zero. When you are acquiring property, you want a high IRR because that means that you need a low present value of the cash flow to achieve the present value of the cash investment. Conversely, when you are selling, you seek a low discount rate because hopefully the present value of the project's cash flow will far exceed the present value of your investment.

Feasibility or Market Study

The problem with the preceding analysis is its simplicity. We assumed a build-to-suit scenario. We assumed we had the building 100 percent preleased prior to the start of construction. Based on our construction costs, we determined what the tenant had to pay as rent in order for us to achieve a 12 percent return on total costs. In this hypothetical example, we can go to the tenant and inquire if $2.23 per square foot per month triple net is an acceptable rent level and, if so, we could possibly finalize a lease on that basis. The problem is in the real world things are usually not so simple. Most of the time at least part of a project is built without knowing who the eventual tenant or tenants will be. Based on the nature of development, it is rare that all of the pieces are in place at commencement of construction. There is a level of preleasing that is necessary to get the project off the ground, but usually 100 percent of the project is not preleased. Additionally, if tenants commit to space up front, often maximum rents cannot be achieved. If a tenant is committing to lease space significantly in advance of the finished product, it usually can negotiate a discount in rent as compared to what the market rent will be once the project is fully built-out. In our example, we knew who the tenant would be, so we would potentially be able to negotiate a rate of $2.23 per square foot per month prior to commencement of construction.

Notwithstanding the above, in the real world, depending on the market, a landlord might have to make concessions in terms of free rent and/or a tenant improvement allowance in excess of the budgeted $50 per square foot amount in the construction costs.

Usually, we might be able to figure out our costs, and we know our target yield, but then we would have to "guesstimate" if we could achieve this rent and how long it will take to lease-up the project. Enter the concept of a feasibility study. The objective of the feasibility study is to determine what rents are achievable and how long it will take to fill the vacant space.

The Composition of a Feasibility Study

A feasibility or market study focusing upon what current competitive rents are is needed to determine if $2.23 per month net, net, net can be achieved and, if so, within what time frame. The study should show what comparable competing space is renting for as well as the vacancy factor in the trade area. Obviously, in order to determine the answers to these questions, you must define what you intend to build and the trade area. The problem is that to some extent the feasibility study is intended to enlighten you as to what you should build, but in order to effectively generate the feasibility study you must make assumptions as to what you are going to build. The reality is that the developer usually has a fairly good idea of what he wants to build going into a project based upon zoning, his past experience, preleasing, and the "logical fit" for the project. Of course, in hindsight a different usage might have been "better" for a site, but that is what makes a ballgame. The point is that the developer's vision of what should be built and the feasibility study are interdependent. The developer's ideas affect the study and the study should influence the final product. Once the product and the location are selected, it can be determined which boundaries should be considered to be within the subject property's competitive market area, and therefore which projects should be scrutinized to determine rent and occupancy levels. Interviews with leasing brokers help to solidify conclusions.

A list of some of the questions that might be asked to generate a feasibility study is shown in Appendix F on the companion website.

Residual Land Value

The preceding fact pattern makes several assumptions: the project cost, the absorption time period, the interest rate that will be charged against the outstanding construction loan balance, and the purchase price of the land.

What if the feasibility study shows that the $26.79 net, net, net annual base rent cannot be achieved? It is possible that you can reduce the project cost, or that the project will lease up in eight months rather than 12 months, or that the interest rate will fall below 7.5 percent. However, it is also possible that the construction costs will exceed the budgeted amount, or that the project will take more than 12 months to achieve stabilized occupancy, or that the prime rate will balloon to 18 percent. In order to construct a rational analysis it is necessary to make realistic assumptions. Nonetheless, if the target yield cannot be achieved based upon the assumed numbers, which variable most likely must give in order to hit the target yield? The answer is the purchase price of the land, since this variable can be controlled.

What value should be ascribed to the land in order to achieve the given yield goal? If we assume our target yield is 12 percent and we can achieve rents of $21 net, net, net, then up to what figure can we afford to pay for the land? A simple formula for determining the applicable project cost would be as follows:

Total Project Cost × 12% = NOI

We know that at $21 base rents, the NOI would be $1,176,000 ($21 × 56,000). Inserting $1,176,000 for NOI and dividing by 12 percent the result is:

Total Project Cost = $9,800,000

Based on our assumptions, the Total Project Cost was $12,500,000. Even if we attribute zero value to the land we still cannot come in at the cost of $9,800,000, which is needed to achieve the target yield. The conclusion is that the project does not meet our yield criteria.

In contrast, if we lower our yield expectations to 8 percent with assumed base rents of $21, the formula results in a maximum acceptable total project cost of $14,700,000. The total project cost based on a land value of $663,050 ($5.00 per square foot on 3.047 acres) was $12,500,000; hence there is plenty of room to negotiate the land price.

This method of determining land value is often referred to as the *residual land value approach*. Essentially, you determine your target value and then working backward, back out all of the hard and soft costs needed to get there. What you are left with is a land value. If value or sales prices decrease and construction costs remain constant, then the amount that you can afford to pay for the land decreases. Similarly, if values or sales prices increase and everything else remains constant, you have more negotiation room in purchasing the land component.

Preleasing

Let us assume that you have completed your due diligence sufficient to conclude that you wish to pursue the project. The site does not have soil issues, the title is clean, and the survey does not reflect any problems with easements, encroachments, or similar matters. You have consulted with an architect and possibly an engineer and have verified what you can build corresponds with what you want to construct. Also, market research has shown that $2.23 per square foot per month is achievable, that there is a strong demand for medical office space, and that the geographic area where the property is located is not "thin," that is, there is a strong demand for medical services and there are several competitive medical buildings and therefore many doctors in the trade area to compete for the available rentable space. Should you start building?

Most commercial projects require some level of preleasing before a construction project should be started. The level of required preleasing is a function of the developer's comfort level, the requirements of his lender and, possibly, based upon input from investors. There is no right answer as to what the proper level of preleasing should be. Should the rents to be generated from the preleased tenants be at least sufficient to cover (1) operating expenses, or (2) operating expenses and the principal and interest obligations, or (3) operating expenses, principal and interest obligations, and a sufficient amount to pay a reasonable return to the investors?

Equity and Financing

In addition to an acceptable level of preleasing, the developer should also have his equity monies lined up. Ideally, the project construction financing should also be in place.

Having adequate reserves is often the key to a successful project. Development contains a lot of unknowns and, therefore, having an adequately funded contingency reserve is very helpful.

Construction financing is typically secured before a spade is placed in the ground. The developer wants to ensure that he has sufficient monies to complete the project. What is more, as mentioned below, mechanics' lien issues arise if work, however small, is started before the construction loan is recorded. Construction financing is typically issued by a bank and is usually structured as full recourse. In addition to the pitfalls of not providing for adequate reserves, success or failure of a development project can be a function of not anticipating and planning for contingencies relating to financing. It is therefore highly recommended that an extension and a miniperm (intermediate loan of three to five years) be built into the loan commitment. No one can know what the economic climate will be when the project is completed. No one has a crystal ball that can foretell whether funding will be readily available or severely constricted, or whether the pricing will be affordable or very expensive. Therefore, building flexibility into the loan in terms of extensions, an intermediate-term additional time frame for the loan, as well as agreed-upon pricing assists the owner in cushioning risk.

Mechanics' Liens

One of the important issues that should be focused on at the outset in conjunction with a construction project is mechanics' liens. Mechanics' liens relate to claims made by contractors and/or subcontractors or other venders who have supplied material or services to the project. In California, as well as many other states, mechanics' liens relate back in priority to the commencement of construction. In other words, if you start construction on January 1 and you record the trust deed for the construction loan on January 10, you have created a potential problem. Any claim for services rendered in July made by a contractor or subcontractor, such as an electrician, relates back to January 1, the beginning of construction, and takes priority over the construction loan. Lenders tend to frown on a loss of priority.

The simple way to avoid this problem is to record the construction loan before any work whatsoever is commenced on the project. Sometimes, however, this orderly process does not work. For example, what do you do if you must start construction to meet a tenant's occupancy needs and the construction lender is not in a position to record? An alternative solution is to work with the title company so that the title company takes the risk on mechanics' lien priority and issues a clean policy to the lender. For the title company to make this accommodation, they will usually insist on an indemnity from the borrower.

Before accepting the indemnity, the title company will want to approve the financial soundness and the creditworthiness of the debtor. If approved, the lender in actuality is in a far superior position after the indemnity than before, since now it has as a contractual obligation to both the title company as well as the borrower, ensuring that there are no mechanics' liens ahead of the lender's loan. The lender, in essence, obtains an additional guarantor relative to this issue. Please note: If the title company does not accept the owner's indemnity (or, as is the case in some states, the title company will not, in any event, write around mechanics' liens), then possibly the lender will accept a performance bond and/or additional collateral.

Liability under the Construction Loan

It is typical for a construction loan to be recourse. The borrower personally guaranties the debt. It is possible, although rare, to obtain a nonrecourse construction loan or to negotiate a cap on your personal exposure. Both the nonrecourse feature and the cap are typically a function of the amount of the borrower's equity in the project. The greater the equity, the more likely the lender will bend on this issue.

Furthermore, a distinction must be made between a *guaranty of completion* and a *guaranty of payment*. Under a guaranty of completion, the borrower is personally liable to complete the project lien free. A guaranty of payment goes beyond this obligation and obligates the borrower to be personally responsible that the loan is paid timely in accordance with the contractual agreement with the lender.

Design and Construction Drawings

Okay, the developer has approved the contingencies in the contract to buy the dirt, has his equity and financing in place, and then closed escrow and purchased the land. The developer, if he has not done so already, must select an architect with whom to work. The choice may be obvious if the developer is seasoned and has successfully worked with a particular architect on this type of project in the past. However, if the developer is starting out or has not developed this type of project before, then a selection process should be established. Face-to-face interviews with candidates are essential. The developer should understand who is going to do the preliminary work, who will do the construction drawings, who will oversee the project to ensure compliance with the plans and specs, and so on. Often, in a large architectural firm, you might meet with the chief architect only to find subordinates actually doing the key work. This might be acceptable, but it should be an informed choice with a possible caveat that the senior partner remains primarily responsible for the services and is required to sign off at all of the crucial steps.

Once an architect is selected, a contract should be entered into. Usually, the American Institute of Architects (AIA) form is utilized. Bear in mind that this agreement is drafted to protect the architect. From the developer's perspective, modifications to the form should be made or a different format might be utilized. For example, the AIA form does not clearly spell out who is hiring the structural and mechanical engineer. Are the engineering fees included within the architect's contract?

The developer must meet with the project architect, since architectural plans and specifications must be drawn as agreed-to between the parties.

Governmental Approvals

In general, before any major work can be done, a permit is required—although it might be permissible to do some minor improvements to the site first. For example, at times, a municipality may issue a grading permit over the counter without full plans and specifications, but this is an exception rather than the rule. In most jurisdictions, the time frame to obtain governmental approval for a new project has increased over the last few decades. Residential projects can take years; commercial approval is usually measured in months, that is, usually three to six months.

Development is tied into governmental approvals. The nature of what can be built, as well as specific zoning regulations, access rules, permissible use, set backs, density, height restrictions, parking requirements, floor/area ratios (FAR), hours of operation, and so on are all a function of the applicable codes and of what the planning commission and city counsel will allow. If you desire to build a project, it is therefore crucial, if at all possible, to establish a working relationship with the local homeowners associations and other citizen groups as well as with city planners, the city manager, the city attorney, and the members of the city counsel. Having a dialogue with and listening to the needs and desires of these key players is very helpful in achieving what you desire to accomplish. Litigation, although unfortunately all too common in residential development, is infrequent in a commercial ground-up project. Needless to say, creating a dialogue, being a good listener, and compromising all go a long way toward avoiding litigation.

Complications often arise when a developer seeks a variance or a conditional use permit. In other words, issues often occur when the developer asks the applicable governmental entity to approve an exception to the stated codes and rules. Typical concerns of the planning commission or city counsel usually revolve around interrelated areas of congestion, parking, noise, traffic, fumes, environmental concerns, and the like.

Environmental issues have become more and more prevalent over the years. Residential development usually feels the greatest impact; however, commercial development may also be impacted, especially if the development is to be located in an environmentally sensitive area, such as wetlands. If environmental issues surface, the developer may be required to commission an environmental impact study (EIS) or even possibly an environmental impact report (EIR). These studies are intended to show the impact of the development on public services such as roads, schools, the police force, fire stations, and utilities such as water, sewer, and electric power. A full EIR might further reflect the development's potential impact on traffic, congestion, local vegetation, air quality, archaeology, animal habitat, and so on.

Very often, the negotiation process boils down to trading for a variance in return for delivering what the various opposition parties or approval entities deem desirable. If I dedicate open space for a park, will the counsel allow me to build an additional 50,000 square feet? If I give $25,000 in free parking validations, will the mayor vote to allow me to charge for parking? Assume a project is zoned for office usage. What if the office market has a high vacancy factor, but the medical office market is still robust. The trick is to determine what concessions must be made to allow a portion of the project to be approved for medical office usage. Assume your project is in a redevelopment area. You want to obtain a matching fund grant from the city. City counsel elections are coming up next quarter. Who you support and whose election you work for could have a huge impact on whether you will obtain a grant and on the amount of that grant. It is not uncommon for governmental approvals, especially in times of economic stress, to be conditioned upon the developer paying impact fees and/or making significant improvements to the area's infrastructure. Typically, street access to the project and possibly freeway on-ramp or off-ramp improvements might be conditions for approval.

Covenants, Conditions, and Restrictions (CC&Rs)

In addition to the governmental codes and rules that affect a property, the developer or the owner of a project might have recorded *covenants, conditions, and restrictions* (CC&Rs) that might affect the development. These CC&Rs supplement code. To the extent that a CC&R violates an existing law, it is not enforceable. An obvious example of this would be a racial or religious restriction. It would be unenforceable for a CC&R to bar people of a certain race or religion from being a tenants in a retail or office project. However, wide latitude is given to other restrictions that do not run afoul of the law. CC&Rs might prohibit specific usages and goods that can be sold. They might also dictate who manages the property, its hours of operation, permissible delivery areas, and so forth. The main point is that if a development opportunity is contemplated, the CC&Rs should be read and thoroughly understood prior to moving forward with the project.

Ground Lease Restrictions

Similar to CC&Rs, restrictions might be found in a ground lease that affects the property to be built prior, during, and after construction. For example, it is common for a hospital to control the land surrounding the hospital campus. If the hospital and the developer seek to enter into a ground lease with the objective being for the developer to then build a medical office building on the land (to the hospital's and developer's mutual benefit), the developer must be careful to scrutinize what, if any, restrictions the hospital imposes. It is common for the hospital to seek to avoid competition by providing that, for example, all tenants in the contemplated medical building be medical doctors on the hospital's staff. It is also possible that certain uses might be prohibited; for example, a surgical center, physical and occupational therapy, or imaging (including MRI, CAT scan, X-ray, etc.). The developer should be primarily concerned, especially in light of these restrictions, that he may not be able to completely lease the building. To address the developer's fear, a compromise might be drafted to provide that in the event the building is less than a certain percentage leased after a certain time frame, some or all of the restrictions might be lifted.

Construction of Improvements in a Ground-Up Development

When hiring a general contractor, it is important to interview several prospects. As in any hiring process, it is helpful to obtain references, but I have never had a prospect give me a bad reference. The most important question is one you ask of yourself: Do you feel you can get along with this individual?—since the construction process is usually long and involves interfacing with the contractor often in terms of decisions that must be made. Fostering a dialogue that results in good communication is paramount.

Another key question to ask is how the general contractor works in terms of staffing versus contracting out various services. Does the general contractor have a crew that performs some or all or the work, and to what extent does the general contractor use subcontractors? There is not necessarily a negative taint on billing out some or all of the work to other parties, but the key is to know what you are getting. By meeting with several contractors and obtaining bids from those parties, you will be able to compare costs and quality. Your education starts with inspecting and comparing the bids and asking why the line item for a specific trade, for example, carpentry, is so much higher here than in the other bid? Is it because one bid is based upon custom cabinetry while the other is based on off-the-shelf items from a hardware supply store? If the painting bids differ dramatically, does that mean that one party is using their in-house personnel while the other party is planning to use a painting contractor?

Who will be the on-site construction manager for the contractor? The manager is a key player and therefore his experience level and demeanor are crucial. Who are the subcontractors that the general contractor plans to use? The answer to these and other questions are crucial.

When reviewing the construction contract, there are three key areas to focus on, namely:

1. Payment. How is the payment to be structured? Does the contract envision a fixed priced amount or a time and materials agreement? Most agreements specify a maximum cost. Otherwise the developer is exposing himself to unknown, unlimited costs. The exception is when the job is so uncertain that a fixed price cannot be given without exposing the general contractor to significant unknown risks. A hybrid contract might set forth time and material with a maximum. Another way to structure the contract is to fix the general contractor's fee and agree that the general contractor will work with the developer to supervise, price out, and hire all of the subcontractors. In a sense, under this arrangement, the contractor becomes, at least for this job, more like an employee of the developer. Under this arrangement, to create an incentive, the developer might agree to give the general contractor a bonus contingent upon completing the project under budget.

2. Timing. Time is money. How long a project takes to complete from grading to finishes is usually a critical element in the success or failure of a project. If the developer plans to come on line with his shopping center in the first quarter of the year, and if the project is delayed so it comes on stream toward the end of the year, that could have serious negative consequences. Financing rates might have increased dramatically or funding might no longer be readily available, or other competing projects completed during the delay might have captured a major portion of the targeted tenants, or the end of the year sale period—when retailers are more likely to enter into leases to capture this high-volume opportunity—might be missed.

3. Final payment. Assume the owner has held back 10 percent of the contract amount to be disbursed upon final completion, that is, issuance of a certificate of occupancy for the building. Is this adequate protection for the owner? Probably, it is not. There also must be a provision that indicates that funds will not be disbursed until all mechanics' liens are cleared. This is the standard that most contracts follow. I suggest, however, that additional protections for the owner should be built into the contract as a condition to final payment. Additional conditions should include obtaining an agreement from the contractor that all subcontractors will be paid in full. At times, a vendor who is owed money may not have taken the proper legal precaution to file a mechanics' lien. If they have a claim and have not filed a mechanics' lien and the contract between the developer and the contractor merely says, "if there are no mechanics' liens, then the owner must pay the contractor," the owner has no recourse but to honor the contract and pay the contractor in full. Litigation is likely to result. Also, the developer might consider including an indemnity provision into the agreement requiring the general contractor to indemnify and hold the owner harmless from any claims or causes of action from any subcontractor relating to the project. Furthermore, the contract should require the general contractor to deliver a list of all of the subcontractors who were involved in the project, detailing their involvement. The list can act as a handy reference if and when problems arise that must be addressed and it can also help to identify the contact parties for applicable warranties.

Inspections

Let us assume that your plans and specifications (P&S) have been completed, and that they have gone through the planning committee and all required modifications have been made. The P&S have also passed through all of the applicable city departments, such as the building department and the fire department. The controversial matters went before the city counsel and acceptable compromises were worked out. You have hired a construction company and it has started to build the improvements. Now your general contractor is in the process of putting up drywall for the central corridor and a city building inspector says, "This doesn't work, you need to have a fire-rated wall here with the drywall going to the ceiling." Your contractor responds "The P&S have been reviewed by your fire department and fully approved. The P&S do not call for a fire-rated wall here, just three-quarter inch dry wall."

The reality is that approval of the P&S is a conditional approval. It is conditional on interpretation of the applicable code provisions and subject to the city changing its mind. At some point in time, there is justifiable reliance on the part of the developer, but, in general, the developer remains subject to an inspector saying that, regardless of the prior approvals, a modification is required. As with other governmental officials, it is helpful to maintain a good working relationship with the city inspectors.

In addition to city building inspectors verifying that the build-out is being done per code, the construction lender will usually require an inspection prior to disbursement of funds. Draw requests are tied to completion of certain work. The lender wants to satisfy itself that the work represented has been completed.

Both the city building inspector and the lender's inspection company can be helpful to the sponsor in terms of pointing out problem areas that might need correction or areas that should be focused on to ensure that the build-out will not lead to problems down the road. However, a prudent developer will usually take additional precautionary steps and contract with experts to protect his interest. Most often, the architect is employed to check up on the project as it progresses to verify that it is being built according to the plans and specifications. The problem is that, in the real world, if the architect comes once a week to the site, it is a blessing. The point is that the architect's review is typically cursory. Depending on the size and scope of the project, it is wise for the developer to hire various experts at different stages of the development to ensure a quality outcome. For example, when the soil is being compacted, you might hire a company to verify that it has been properly compacted. When the foundation is being poured, an engineer should be hired to certify that it is level and properly placed and reinforced. While the framing, electric, and plumbing are being installed, you might retain a former building inspector or another general contractor to check up on the process to ensure that you are not being short-changed, and so on.

Insurance

During construction, the owner must maintain builder's risk insurance. He should also provide in the construction contract that the contractor and all subcontractors maintain workmen's compensation, general liability, and builder's risk insurance. The owner should be named as an additional insured on the general liability and builder's risk coverage. The problem is that contracting and requiring this coverage and actually securing the coverage are two different things. Assuming you are working with a reliable professional general contractor, you can expect to secure the applicable proof of insurance from this party, especially since you can hold up payment until the documentation arrives. The breakdown usually occurs in relation to the subcontractors. Some of the subcontractors will supply the requested documentation, but since their relationship is primarily with the general contractor, not the owner, it is much more difficult to obtain evidence of compliance from the subcontractors.

There is a clear differentiation in insurance requirements demanded by small to medium-size firms and large or institutional companies. The large or institutional companies commonly require coverage of at least $1 million per occurrence, $2 million aggregate, and $5 million excess. The result is often to eliminate potential contractors or subcontractors and clearly to increase the cost of construction.

Decisions, Decisions, Decisions

A ground-up construction project consists of making a thousand-plus decisions from the big picture to minute details. Appendix G, on the companion website, attempts to break down the decision process into the broad construction categories and then covers some of the big picture issues that must be resolved within the subcategories. I refer to Appendix G as a "Construction Decision Tree." The trunk or major issues leads to branches or minor issues that leads to smaller stems or more detailed concerns. In addition to highlighting major areas that must be addressed, Appendix G also focuses on Code-required areas such as building height or City-required landscaping or lighting. Furthermore, Appendix G attempts to point out some of the sensitive areas that are often overlooked and if so, may create serious problems in the future such as a failure to install separate electric meters for tenants that have equipment with heavy energy usage or the lack of planning for water shut-off values in dental offices so as to avoid after-hour breaks that might relate to dental equipment that could result in major flooding. A comprehensive outline of all of the potential decisions that might have to be addressed is beyond the scope of this text, but Appendix G on the companion website sets forth a rough outline of the major areas wherein decisions of construction type or other concerns must be addressed.

The developer must also be conscious that during the construction process, team members, that is, the architect, the contractor, and various vendors, may make decisions that affect the project without consulting with the owner. The developer must be diligent and focused on the project, since he wants to ensure that key decisions are not made without his knowledge and consent. I do not mean to suggest the decisions are going to be intentionally made in a "Machiavellian" style behind the developer's back, but rather, in the ordinary course of getting things done, frequently decisions will be undertaken extemporaneously. If the developer is not involved in the day-to-day process, many of these decisions will get past him.

Some of the one-thousand-plus decisions include:

How large will the building be? What kind of parking lots or structures will there be? How many parking spaces should be planned for? How many and where should the handicap parking spaces be located? What shall be the architectural style of the project? What building materials should be used? Is the building going to be wood frame with stucco, concrete tilt-up, brick, steel, and glass, or an all-metal structure? What will be the exterior paint color? What shall the exterior skin be composed of: stucco, brick, glass, and so forth? How many elevators will the building contain? Are they electric or hydraulic? What will the landscaping theme be? What type of signage will the project have? Will there be a pylon or a monument sign or both? Will the HVAC units be individual units or one system for the entire building? Where will HVAC units be placed? What should be the roof composition: clay tile, concrete tile, composition, or metal? Should the roof be sloped, flat, or sloped in part and flat in part? Should the windows open in or out or be such that they cannot be opened at all? Is solar paneling a viable alternative or is it more cost-efficient to apply a white coating to the roof surface to reduce energy cost? What style of the plumbing fixtures will be in the common area bathrooms? What type of lighting is the project going to have? What kind of hot water system will the project contain? What shall be the composition of the flooring in the common areas: carpet, hardwood, tile, vinyl, marble, or a combination thereof? What type of security system should the project contain? Should the security system be the landlord's concern or solely a concern of the applicable tenants? Are there any privacy issues, for example, requiring locked cabinets or above standard insulation?

The list of decisions to be made goes on and on. Some of the decisions are made based upon style preference. Other decisions are dictated by cost. Then again, the applicable building code may be the controlling factor. Other choices will be determined by the physical constraints of the site. Regardless, the point is that, in general, there is a lot of leeway for key decisions to be made by the developer. Some of these decisions are largely aesthetic and some can have a direct bearing on the project's economics. If, for example, your intention is to have modified gross or triple net leases in which utilities are billed directly to the tenants, constructing separate electric meters is preferable. It is exponentially harder and usually cost-prohibitive to construct separate meters after the building is built. Despite the sheer volume of decision making required, my point is that all your decisions should be reasoned, informed, and coordinated rather than haphazard choices that occur by default.

Communication, Communication, Communication

The key to a successful ground-up construction project is communication. The communication starts with the developer and the architect. The developer must, as clearly as possible, convey his vision of what he wishes to accomplish to the architect and then the architect must, as a design and plans develop, show the developer as clearly as possible how his vision is being translated into form and function. Communication with the architect is crucial, and this communication occurs not only at the design stage but also beyond, for typically the architect is retained to follow the construction project through from grading to finish, ensuring that the plans and specifications are being followed. The architect must then communicate with all of the other professionals involved in the development process and especially with the engineers: structural, mechanical, electrical, and civil. In addition, it is critical to maintain a dialogue between the developer and the general contractor and/or the on-site job foreman, if applicable. It is important to have frequent site visits to verify the work is going as intended. Depending on the nature of the project, the site visits may be monthly, weekly, or even daily. Problems are bound to arise. The owner should be consulted on the solution alternatives with regard to cost, timing, and method, so that an informed decision may be made.

> ## Rule Number 23
> The key to a successful ground-up construction project is communication.

Graphic Time Line

Usually, at the outset of a construction project, the general contractor will outline a rough time line for the project in graphic form. Exhibit 9.2 provides a sample time line for a project similar to that discussed in this chapter: namely, construction of a two-story medical office building of about 60,000 square feet with parking on grade. The time line divides the project into major categories, that is, preconstruction, site work, building shell, and tenant improvement work, and shows how in the dynamics of construction, the categories are interwoven. For example, it illustrates how, in practice, site work is usually being worked on concurrent with construction of the building structure.

Exhibit 9.2 **Construction Time Table Graph**

MOB PRELIMINARY SCHEDULE—January 1, 2010

ID	Task Name	Duration	Start JAN	Finish
1	**Pre-construction**	**46 days**	Fri 1/1/10	Mon 3/29/10
2	Award Structure Steel to Subcontractor	1 day	Fri 1/1/10	Fri 1/1/10
3	Steel Lead Time	45 days	Mon 1/4/10	Mon 3/29/2010
4	Order Elevator	1 day	Tue 1/5/10	Tue 1/5/10
5	Building Shell Permit	1 day	Tue 1/5/10	Tue 1/5/10
6	Grading Permit Issued	1 day	Tue 1/5/10	Tue 1/5/10
7	Steel/Foundation Permit Issued	1 day	Tue 1/5/10	Tue 1/5/10
8	**Earthwork**	**5 days**	Mon 2/1/10	Fri 2/3/10
9	Clear Site	2 days	Mon 2/1/10	Tue 2/2/10
10	Building Pad Finish Grade	3 days	Mon 2/1/10	Wed 2/3/10
11	**Site Work—Perimeter Parking**	**93 days**	Tue 2/2/10	Fri 4/9/10
12	Driveway Curb Cuts and Demo	5 days	Tue 2/2/10	Mon 2/8/10
13	Site Sewer Line	15 days	Mon 2/15/10	Fri 3/5/10
14	Perimeter Site Curbs	5 days	Mon 2/15/10	Fri 3/19/10
15	Remaining Site Utilities	30 days	Mon 2/15/10	Fri 3/26/10
16	Light Pole Bases for Parking Aisles	10 days	Mon 3/1/10	Fri 3/12/10
17	Landscaping Fine Grade	3 days	Tue 3/16/10	Thur 3/18/10
18	Concrete Paving	10 days	Tue 3/16/2010	Mon 3/29/2010
19	Landscaping	15 days	Tue 3/23/10	Fri 4/9/10
20	**Building Shell**	**203 days**	Tue 3/2/10	Wed 9/23/10
21	Below Grade Utilities	5 days	Tue 3/2/10	Mon 3/8/10
22	Foundations Interior	10 days	Mon 3/8/10	Fri 3/19/10
23	Foundations 1st Floor Level	10 days	Tue 3/23/10	Mon 4/5/10
24	Floating Drain	5 days	Fri 4/9/10	Thur 4/15/10
25	Slab on grade 1st Floor Level	5 days	Wed 3/24/10	Tue 3/30/2010
26	Erect Structural Steel	15 days	Mon 4/24/10	Tue 4/13/10
27	Complete Welding	10 days	Tue 4/13/10	Mon 4/26/10
28	Metal Deck 1st Floor	3 days	Wed 4/14/10	Fri 4/16/10
29	Metal Deck 2nd A30Floor	3 days	Fri 4/16/10	Tue 4/20/10
30	Concrete on Metal Deck 1st Floor	5 days	Fri 4/16/10	Thur 4/20/10
31	Fireproofing 1st Floor	5 days	Thur 4/22/10	Mon 4/28/10
32	Concrete on Metal Deck 2nd Floor	5 days	Mon 4/28/10	Tue 5/4/10
33	Fireproofing 2nd Floor	5 days	Tue 5/4/10	Mon 5/10/10
34	Metal Deck—Flat Roof	4 days	Mon 5/10/10	Fri 5/14/10
35	Concrete on Flat Roof	5 days	Fri 5/14/10	Thur 5/20/10
36	Scaffold Exterior	3 days	Mon 5/10/10	Wed 5/12/10
37	Exterior Wall Framing	30 days	Wed 5/12/10	Tue 6/22/10

#	Task	Duration	Start	Finish
38	Exterior Wall Pluming Rough	2 days	Tue 6/22/10	Wed 6/23/10
39	Exterior Wall Electrical Rough	2 days	Tue 6/22/10	Wed 6/23/10
40	Build Up Roof	10 days	Tue 6/22/10	Wed 7/7/10
41	Exterior Well Sheathing	5 days	Tue 6/22/10	Mon 6/28/10
42	Exterior Lath	10 days	Fri 7/9/10	Thur 7/22/10
43	Scratch and Brown Coat	10 days	Thur 7/22/10	Wed 8/4/10
44	Exterior Glazing	35 days	Wed 7/4/10	Tue 9/21/10
45	Color Coat	3 days	Mon 8/16/10	Wed 8/18/10
46	Scaffold Removal	2 days	Tue 9/21/10	Wed 9/23/10
47	**Interior Common Areas & Tenant Improvements**	**216 days**	Wed 9/23/10	1/14/w11
48	HVAC Rough	10 days	Wed 10/19/10	Mon 11/1/10
49	Stud Framing	20 days	Wed 10/19/10	Mon 11/15/10
50	Blocking	5 days	Wed 10/19/10	Mon 11/1/10
51	Fire Rough In	5 days	Wed 10/19/10	Mon 11/1/10
52	One Side Drywall	10 days	Mon 11/1/10	Fri 11/12/10
53	Electrical Rough In	20 days	Wed 10/19/10	Fri 11/12/10
54	Plumbing Wall Rough In	30 days	Wed 10/19/10	Fri 11/26/10
55	Insulation Interior	2 days	Fri 11/26/10	Mon 11/29/10
56	Plumbing Overhead Rough	5 days	Tue 11/30/10	Mon 12/6/10
57	Bectrical Overhead Rough	5 days	Tue 11/30/10	Mon 12/6/10
58	Fire Marshall Hydro	1 day	Mon 12/6/10	Tue 12/7/10
59	Two Side Drywall	15 days	Wed 10/19/10	Mon 11/8/10
60	Ceilding Grid	7 days	Fri 12/3/10	Mon 12/13/10
61	Prime	5 days	Mon 12/13/10	Fri 12/17/10
62	Paint	10 days	Fri 12/17/10	Thur 12/23/10
63	Sprinkler Trim	5 days	Fri 12/17/10	Fri 12/23/10
64	Interior Doors	5 days	Fri 12/17/10	Fri 12/23/10
65	Ceiling Tile	5 days	Fri 12/17/10	Fri 12/23/10
66	HVAC Trim	3 days	Thur 12/23/10	Thur 12/23/10
67	Hardware	3 days	Thur 12/23/10	Mon 12/27/10
68	Electric Trim and Fixtures	5 days	Thur 12/23/10	Mon 12/27/10
69	Store Front Doors	5 days	Thur 12/23/10	Wed 12/29/10
70	HVAC Start	3 days	Mon 12/27/10	Wed 12/29/10
71	Tile	7 days	Thur 12/23/10	Fri 12/31/10
72	Millwork Install	7 days	Thur 12/23/10	Fri 12/31/10
73	Accessories	5 days	Fri 12/31/10	Thur 1/6/11
74	Plumbing Trim	3 days	Fri 12/31/10	Wed 1/5/11
75	Carpet	3 days	Fri 12/31/10	Wed 1/5/11
76	Certificate of Occupancy	0 days	Wed 1/5/11	Wed 1/7/11
77	Final Clean	2 days	Wed 1/5/11	Fri 1/7/11
78	Fixtures and Furnishings Install	5 days	Fri 1/7/11	Thur 1/13/11
79	Tenants Go Live Date	0 days	Fri 1/14/11	Fri 1/14/11

Timing of construction is a key element in the success or failure of a project. Delays in construction are costly in terms of interest carry and can be detrimental in that a prolonged time frame can potentially result in negative changed circumstances and intervening consequences or events.

The interest carry is obviously a cost tied into timing. The longer a project takes to complete before tenants can be put in place and income generated, the greater the loan interest expense is not set off by rents.

There are many negative consequences that may result from delays—some subtle, some direct and obvious. For example, assume a project is scheduled to be completed in four months; however, six weeks into construction, the majority of the work still remains unfinished. Let us say a major hurricane hits the Gulf States, causing a severe shortage of raw materials. The result is that oil prices and the cost of building materials, such as sheetrock and lumber, skyrocket. Alternatively, assume that a large 1,000-unit apartment building is in the framing stage. A fire destroys the complex. The developer rebuilds, but the fire results in a 10-month delay. During the downtime, another large competitive apartment project has been completed. The result is that leasing concessions such as free rent must be offered to prospective tenants in order to induce them to rent from our project rather than our competitor's project and the lease-up time frame has been significantly compromised.

To some extent, steps can be taken to protect against the cost of delays. If the contractor agrees, penalties can be imposed against the contractor if the project is not timely completed. Nonetheless, even if the contractor agrees to a penalty, logically there should be exceptions for acts of God and any other events outside of the contractor's control. Also, if the construction contract sets forth a downside, a penalty for failure to deliver substantial completion before a certain date, then possibly the contractor should be rewarded for bringing in the project early.

Project Operating Costs

When preparing a construction budget, developers plan for contingencies in both hard and soft costs, but often they do not anticipate the problem of carrying a project's operating costs if there are significant delays. Costs such as real property taxes and insurance continue, whether or not there is a tenant in occupancy. These costs must be budgeted for.

Lender's Disbursement Form

In order to obtain a disbursement from the construction loan, lenders typically require the borrower to complete a loan disbursement form. The form reflects the line items of the approved construction loan and shows what monies have been disbursed and what still remains to be disbursed. Exhibit 9.3 is an example of a loan disbursement form with numbers filled in for the hypothetical example in this chapter. The key is that the construction loan funds are allocated into categories and if you exhaust that category you must tap the contingency line item, if available. The goal is to, as best as possible, anticipate the possible categories and develop a strong working relationship with your construction loan administrator so that, if necessary, you can shift funds from one category that has not been significantly tapped into a category that requires funding.

Exhibit 9.3 Lender's Disbursement Form

LENDER'S DISBURSEMENT BUDGET & APPLICATION FOR PAYMENT

LOAN #: 457-2009
BORROWER: Medical Office Building, LLC
CONTRACTOR: Reliable Construction, Inc.
PROJECT: Medical Office Building

A	B	C	D	E	F	G
Item #	Description	Initial Project Budget	Previously Approved Changes	Proposed Changes	Adjusted Project Budget (C + D + E)	Costs Paid or to Be Paid by Borrower
1	Land/ Acquisition Cost	$353,773			$353,773.00	$353,773.00
2						
	SUBTOTAL LAND:	$353,773			$353,773.00	$353,773.00
1	Construction Costs Subtotal (Contract)	$3,333,754	$258,306.95		$3,592,061	
4	Tenant Improvements	$1,347,650			$1,347,650	$500,000
5	Contingency (Hard Costs)	$400,000	$(355,506.95)		$44,493	
	SUBTOTAL HARD:	$5,081,404	$(97,200.00)		$4,984,204	$500,000
Construction Soft Costs:						
1	Architectural & Engineering	$113,000			$113,000	$109,250
2	Permit & Gov't Fees	$73,480			$73,480	$28,480
3	Soils Testing	$12,000			$12,000	
4	Legal Fees	$63,500			$63,500	$44,438
5	Leasing Costs	$75,000			$75,000	
6	Contingency (Soft Costs)	$50,597	$97,200.00		$147,797	$42,211
Financing, etc. Soft Costs:						
1	Interest Reserve (Construction)	$367,575			$367,575	

LENDER: The Construction Bank   DATE: _____

REQUEST #: 1

H	I	J	K	L	M	N	O
Costs Paid by Borrower to Date	Costs to Be Paid by Borrower (G – H)	Adjusted Loan Disbursement Budget (F – G)	Loan Percent Disbursed ([M + N] / J)	Adj. Project Budget % Disbursed ([H + M + N] / F)	Previous Loan Disbursements	This Loan Disbursement Request (Net of Retention)	Adj. Undisbursed Loan Budget (J – M – N)
$353,773.00				100.00%			
$353,773.00			0.00%	100.00%			
		$3,592,061	102.20%	102.20%	$3,082,169	239,546.00	$270,345
	$500,000	$847,650	29.49%	18.55%	$249,999		$597,651
		$44,493	6.29%	6.29%	$2,800		$41,693
	$500,000	$4,484,204	79.71%	71.72%	$3,334,969	$239,546.00	$909,689
$109,250		$3,750	100.00%	100.00%	$3,750		
$28,480		$45,000	0.00%	38.76%			$45,000
		$12,000	100.00%	100.00%	$10,671		$1,329
$44,438		$19,062	100.00%	100.00%	$19,062		
		$75,000	0.00%	0.00%			$75,000
$42,211		$105,586	85.90%	89.93%	$89,041	$1,658.00	$14,887
		$367,575	20.31%	20.31%	$74,650		$292,925

A	B	C	D	E	F	G
Item #	Description	Initial Project Budget	Previously Approved Changes	Proposed Changes	Adjusted Project Budget (C + D + E)	Costs Paid or to Be Paid by Borrower
2	Loan Fee	$52,000			$52,000	
3	Title, Recording, & Escrow Expenses	$27,073			$27,073	
4	Appraisal & Review	$4,000			$4,000	
5	Cost Analysis & Review	$1,250			$1,250	
6	Inspections	$3,000			$3,000	
7	Environmental & Review	$500			$500	
	SUBTOTAL SOFT:	$842,975	$97,200.00		$940,175	$224,379
	TOTAL:	$6,278,152			$6,278,152	$1,078,152

You, The Construction Bank, made the construction loan numbered above (the "Loan") to Medical Office Building, LLC, on March 21, 2009

By signing below, we ask you to make a payment of $_____ from the Loan. We certify that the amount requested is now payable and is in accordance with the Construction Loan Agreement we executed for the Loan. We have attached a copy of the contractor's requisition and other requests, copies of bills, and receipts for items we have paid.

According to our records, when you make the payment requested herein you will have paid a total of $_____ from the Loan.

WE CERTIFY THAT THERE HAS BEEN NO CHANGE IN THE PLANS AND SPECIFICATIONS, OR INCREASE IN COSTS, WHICH YOU HAVE NOT APPROVED.

WE ALSO HEREBY ACKNOWLEDGE THAT THIS FORM MAY BE TRANSMITTED ELECTRONICALLY AND THAT IT MAY NOT BE IN A SECURE ENCRYPTED ENVIRONMENT.

Borrower:
Medical Office Building

Authorized Signor   Print Name & Title

H	I	J	K	L	M	N	O
Costs Paid by Borrower to Date	Costs to Be Paid by Borrower (G – H)	Adjusted Loan Disbursement Budget (F – G)	Loan Percent Disbursed ([M + N] / J)	Adj. Project Budget % Disbursed ([H + M + N] / F)	Previous Loan Disbursements	This Loan Disbursement Request (Net of Retention)	Adj. Undisbursed Loan Budget (J – M – N)
		$52,000	100.00%	100.00%	$52,000		
		$27,073	100.00%	100.00%	$27,073		$0
		$4,000	100.00%	100.00%	$4,000		
		$1,250	100.00%	100.00%	$1,250		
		$3,000	0.00%	0.00%			$3,000
		$500	100.00%	100.00%	$500		
$224,379		$715,796	39.63%	54.04%	$281,997	$1,658.00	$432,141
$578,152	$500,000	$5,200,000	74.20%	70.66%	$3,616,966	$241,204.00	$1,341,830

_____   _____
Authorized Signor   Print Name & Title

It is also important to understand the lender's disbursement process. Often, the lender will require a site inspection prior to disbursement of funds. The inspection, if required, could easily add two weeks to the disbursement time frame. In addition, lenders typically will require, prior to disbursement, a conditional lien release from the general contractor. The lien release is issued conditional on receiving valid funds in payment of the submitted invoice.

Change Orders

During the course of construction of most large construction projects, it will either be discovered that an item has not been covered in the contractor's budget or that a correction must be made due to myriad reasons.

The key steps in a change order include (1) verifying that the change order was approved and (2) reviewing the contractor's budget to make sure that the change order was not already included in the budget or, if it was, at what amount. (In other words, if the budget has a $7,500 allowance for hardware and the contractor submits a $9,000 change order for hardware, is the change order in *addition* to the allowance, or does the allowance cover the first $7,500 of the bill with the change order actually covering only $1,500?)

Rehabilitation Project

The initial hypothetical example in this chapter deals with a ground-up construction project. This portion of the text discusses an existing project that requires work to enhance its value. This work can be as simple as a cosmetic facelift, for example, paint, landscaping, and/or paving, or as extensive as a major makeover, for example, a new façade and new structural support columns. The subtitle to the chapter, "Build to a 12 Percent Yield" applies to any project, including a rehabilitation project, wherein value is to be created.

Let us assume that we are considering purchasing a 90,000 square foot shopping center, called The Metro Plaza. The existing rent roll is shown in Exhibit A.7 on the companion website. In the broker's sale package, the income and expense analysis suggests a current NOI of $800,000. (See Exhibit 9.4.)

Exhibit 9.4 **Metro Plaza Income and Expense Analysis**

The Metro Plaza
Tucson, AZ

Income and Expenses

Gross Lease Area (GLA) 90,000 SF	CURRENT	PER SF	PRO FORMA	PER SF
GROSS BASE RENT	$957,245	$10.64	$1,402,535	$15.58
Expense Reimbursements	$134,618	$1.50	$336,023	$3.73
GROSS POTENTIAL INCOME (GPI)	1,091,863	$12.14	$1,738,558	$19.32
Vacancy/Collection Allowance (% of GPI)	*		(5.0%) 86,928	
EFFECTIVE GROSS INCOME	$1,091,863	$12.54	$1,651,630	$18.35
Expenses				
Real Estate Taxes	150,000	1.67	190,000	$3.24
Insurance	25,000	0.28	30,012	0.33
Utilities	13,000	0.14	13,000	0.14
Repairs & Maintenance	70,000	0.78	70,000	0.78
Management Fee	33,863	0.38	33,011	0.37
TOTAL EXPENSES	$291,863	$3.24	$336,023	$3.65
NET OPERATING INCOME	$800,000	$8.89	$1,315,607	$14.62

COMMENTS
*Vacancy is already factored in at 40.50%

How do we decide what to offer for this property? We may find an answer to this question if we go back to the subtitle to this chapter, "Build to a 12 Percent Yield."

Since we have not as yet conducted any due diligence, let us assume that the financial numbers in the sales package are accurate, unless we perceive a modification is needed. The challenge boils down to solving for an unknown, the purchase price, after making assumptions about what the NOI will be at stabilized occupancy, what the cost is to get to stabilized occupancy, and what yield we desire to achieve on our capital.

One way to derive our purchase price would be to work backward, starting with an actual rent roll and making assumptions as to what rent can be achieved during lease up. From there, an income and expense analysis can be composed. This gives us an NOI. We can then figure out the cost to get there ("C"), except the purchase price ("P"). Also, we must decide what an acceptable yield on the Total Costs would be. Let us assume an acceptable yield is 12 percent. Finally, we know that Total Costs equals C plus P. Therefore, we can use the simple algebraic equation Total Costs × 12 percent = NOI or C + P × 12 percent = NOI. Dividing each side by 12 percent results in C + P = NOI/12 percent. We can now solve for the purchase price. The final step is to take the derived Total Cost number and back out all known costs, which results in a plug number: the purchase price.

This process can be summarized in five steps as follows:

Step 1: Determine realistic, achievable income numbers.

Step 2: Determine realistic, achievable expense numbers.

Step 3: Derive NOI.

Step 4: Determine FMV at the acceptable cap rate to which you are developing the project given project risk, effort, *etc.*

Step 5: Back out the estimated costs to achieve the pro forma lease-up to determine the purchase price.

Applying the above to our hypothetical example, the result is as follows:

Step 1: Gross income equals the income set forth in Exhibit 9.4 plus the rent increase soon to take effect for the chiropractic office plus the vacant space at the scheduled rate per square foot. The existing owners have been unable to lease-up the vacant space, so our thinking is that to lease-up this space, a significant discount from the rent being achieved on the rented space is necessary. In reviewing rent comparables for the area, it is determined that at the scheduled rent per square foot number, the vacant space can be rented over a two-year time frame. This results in a total gross income of $1,402,623.

Step 2: For purposes of this analysis, we are going to accept the sales package's estimated total expenses of $336,023.

Step 3: Derive NOI:

Gross Income	$1,402,623
Less Expense Reimbursements	336,023
Total Gross Income	$1,738,558
Less Vacancy and Collection Loss	86,928
Effective Gross Income	$1,651,630
Less Operating Expenses	336,023
Net Operating Income	$1,315,607

Step 4: We must decide now what yield do we want to achieve when the project is complete? Again, the project subtitle says "Build to a 12 Percent

Yield." The subject project is not a ground-up development project. It is already in existence, but, depending on the project's scope, we may still have to contend with many of the risks associated with constructing the project from ground up including, without limitation, the permit process, delays due to weather, neighboring homeowners' issues, material cost variations, and so on. However, let us assume the project location is a "B" to "C" area, the leasing market is very soft, and, given the occupancy of the project, any financing will most likely have to be full recourse. We therefore decide to "Build to a 11.5 Percent Yield." Hence, the fair market value at completion is estimated to be $11,440,061 ($1,315,607/.115).

Step 5: We must now back-out the cost to achieve this value. Appendix H on the companion website reflects an analysis of the estimated costs to achieve the lease up of the project. Therefore, reducing the FMV at completion by the cost to get there results in a purchase price of $9,363,672 ($11,404,607 − 2,076,389). Based upon this purchase price, the going-in cap rate would be 8.54 percent ($800,000 NOI/$9,363,672 purchase price) and the cost per square foot would be $104 ($9,363,672 purchase price/90,000 square feet).

Construction of Improvements in a Rehab Project: Decisions, Decisions, Decisions

As in a ground-up construction project, a thousand-plus decisions must be made during the course of the rehabilitation project and often the decisions are made on a daily, if not hourly, basis.

Rehab Project: Communication, Communication, Communication

Similar to the dynamics of a ground-up construction project, the success or failure of a rehabilitation project often turns on the developer's ability to communicate with the various parties involved. Usually, communication is even more important and difficult in a rehab project because additional parties are involved. It is common in a rehabilitation project to keep part of the project open for business. Therefore, the developer, in addition to the normal coordination with the general contractor, the architect, the surveyor, various subcontractors, and so on must also be concerned with tenants and guests. In a construction project, there are always safety concerns, but the concerns are amplified to the extent existing tenants and their patrons are involved.

Summary

As a general rule a ground-up construction project and a rehabilitation project is more difficult, more complicated, and more risky than a straight acquisition of an existing leased project. However, with risk there is usually more potential reward. Additional elements that you must be concerned with in a development or a rehab project include project feasibility, design, governmental approvals, and, of course, construction.

To assess a development or a rehabilitation project, start with a target yield, determine the project's estimated cost, pro forma income, and expenses at stabilized occupancy, and then work backward to find what you can afford to pay for the land in a ground-up development project or the project in a rehab transaction.

Be aware that decisions must be made constantly in a successful development or rehab project and therefore the developer's continuing involvement is crucial. Also communication is important to a successful project between the developer and the architect, the developer and the contractor, the contractor and the architect, and so on.

CHAPTER 10

Marketing, Leasing, and Management

When I first thought about how best to present the subjects of marketing, leasing, and management, I considered writing three separate chapters. Upon reflection, I felt that these subjects were so intertwined, or *should* be so intertwined, that one chapter discussing all three subjects would be much more helpful.

Definition of Marketing, Leasing, and Management

What do I mean by "marketing, leasing, and management"? My definition of marketing is a broad one, including both the process to attract new tenants through promotion of the project as well as that of encouraging patrons to buy goods or services from existing tenants, thereby stimulating their business and making the overall project more viable. Leasing refers to the steps that must be taken that culminate in signing a contractual agreement with a potential tenant, existing or new, wherein the tenant gains the right to use and enjoy the subject premises in return for paying rent. In other words, leasing means filling vacancies with new tenants or renewing existing lease obligations. Management is the day-to-day running of a property: everything from fixing the toilet to painting the exterior of the structure to addressing tenant complaints or concerns, and monitoring the tenants' timely payment of rent.

Why are these three subjects intertwined? Effective marketing leads to increased leasing, but also should lead to consummating renewals and, hopefully, to tenant referrals that fill vacancies. A good leasing and management team reduces the need for marketing. A key element in marketing should be to show that a great property management team is in place. The objective is to communicate that the subject project is a good environment from which to run a business, since in addition to its attractive location and other benefits, there are both a property manager in particular and a property administration in general that are fair and reasonable and will work with the lessee to solve any problems that might arise.

The most expensive costs in running a property are often the costs surrounding the loss of a tenant. The consequences of losing a tenant include downtime, that is, rents that are lost while the unit is being marketed for a new occupant, as well as potential additional costs associated with legal fees, brokerage commissions, and tenant improvement dollars. The statement that "the most expensive costs in running a property are the costs surrounding loss of a tenant" is mitigated, of course, by situations when the demands of an existing tenant are unreasonable from the landlord's standpoint and when, therefore, it is better to start afresh by negotiating with a new prospective lessee. Such a circumstance, however, should be the exception, not the rule.

> ### Rule Number 24
> The most expensive costs in running a property are the costs surrounding the loss of a tenant. Unless their demands are unreasonable, keep an existing tenant happy, because, in general, it is far more expensive to replace that tenant.

Marketing

What should marketing a real estate project entail? Of course, the scope of the assignment has a direct relationship with the nature of the property and the extent of the vacant space that must be leased. A game plan must be thought out and preferably committed to paper.

Historically, marketing has been conducted by the landlord or a marketing association, or in conjunction with a marketing fund. Usually, the marketing association or the marketing fund is controlled by the landlord since it is funded by contributions from the tenants and the landlord, typically on a matching fund basis. Marketing associations are uncommon today, since the same objectives can be accomplished through a marketing fund without negative tax repercussions. Even marketing funds are rare. They are usually found in larger shopping centers where the landlord has had the bargaining power to build this obligation into all of the leases because of the desirability of the property. Retailers are usually resistant to contributing to such a fund since they are sensitive to increasing their expense line items and they argue that they already are expending monies directed at marketing their stores. For purposes of this section, it is assumed that the landlord will be the sole active player in marketing the property and conducting any and all efforts to market in an attempt to secure new or replacement tenants.

Let's assume we have just acquired Crossroads Plaza, a 120,000-square-foot shopping center with 7,800 square feet of vacancy, that is, vacancies that constitute 6.5 percent of the project. Most of the vacant space is composed of 1,300-square-foot shop spaces, some of which are contiguous and some of which are separated by leased space. Let us also assume that the 20,000-square-foot anchor space is occupied by the Giant Green Grocer, a national market with only two years to go on its lease. The anchor tenant is losing money and has indicated that, based on the store's current performance, it is not intending to renew the lease. The Center also has an undeveloped outpad upon which a building of about 5,000 square feet could be constructed. A current rent roll can be viewed on the companion website as Exhibit A.8.

Marketing Game Plan

The first step should be to lay out a written game plan, a strategy for promoting the Center and leasing-up the vacancy. The game plan can be a narrative or a series of simple bullet points hitting the main areas of focus. The game plan should be site specific. In other words, making nice statements like "We are going to work hard to fill all of the vacancy" really does not achieve the objective. Rather, specifics are needed. For example, in our hypothetical, we know that the anchor will probably not renew its lease. Therefore, an analysis should be made to determine the feasibility and cost associated with breaking up the 20,000-square-foot vacant space. Does this size space work for a traditional supermarket such as Albertson's or Von's, or should the premises, given its size, be presented to upscale "niche" specialty markets such as Trader Joe's or RJ's?

There is no single correct format for the marketing plan, and since each marketing plan is site specific, no two marketing plans will be the same. Subject matters that might be covered in the marketing plan include:

- The project's existing characteristics: It is important to understand what you have to work with.
- Demand generators: Why do shoppers come to this shopping center? Is it due to the proximity to their home or business?
- What is in the immediate area surrounding the center and how does it affect the subject property?
- General market knowledge: If a specific tenant is a good candidate for your center but already has a store across the street, you can probably eliminate this prospect; however, if this tenant's lease is expiring and your center is a superior location and tenant mix, perhaps it jumps to the top of your prospect list.
- What are the goals, short-and long-range, that the owner seeks to accomplish?
- Strategies and tactics to accomplish the goals.
- Specific action items to carry out the strategies and tactics. (See also Chapter 1, including Exhibit 1.1.)

Existing Center's Characteristics

The obvious starting point is to analyze what you have. Understand your existing center. Ask three key questions: What are the existing tenants like? What is missing from the center? What are the physical characteristics that define this center? In other words, scrutinize the type of tenants you have and this property's place in the world. Do the existing tenants sell commodities, or is the center more of a service center, providing professional advice to the community, or a combination of the two? To illustrate, a discount store and a supermarket sell goods; in contrast, a dance or karate studio, an income tax consultant, an insurance agent, a chiropractor, and a dentist sell services.

Make a list of what services or stores the center may be missing. For example, if the center is a service-oriented center, does it have a hair or nail salon or dry cleaners? Is there a type of tenant that is missing that is normally associated with the anchor tenant? For example, a movie theater often has in close proximity a coffee shop, a food court, or an ice-cream store. Is there food service in close proximity to the theater? Can the food service be expanded?

Last, concentrate on the nature of the vacant space and how the center is physically laid out. For ease of reference, its best to generate a vacancy chart. The center's site plan might be used to reflect vacant units and the corresponding square footage. Can the vacant space be split up? If it can be divided, where is the logical division line and what usable spaces result? What is the depth of the shop space? Is this depth practicable? Are the shops rectangular or cut into odd shapes? What is the parking situation in relationship to the businesses? Is there a standard configuration, with parking in the front of the street and shop space in the back facing the street? Is there adequate parking? Is the parking convenient surface parking or must some of the customers valet park or park in a subterranean garage? How many stories does the center have? Is there an issue with second-story accessibility? Is signage clear or is it hard to locate certain tenants? Is there a visibility issue? Do some of the buildings on the outpads block in-line store signage?

Demand Generators

What are the demand generators for the project? What drives this center? Why do people shop there? Where do the existing tenants derive their business from? Do people come to this center because of its convenience or is it a "destination" center? Is it a neighborhood center or does it draw from a greater geographic area? Does the center have mostly national tenants, local businesses, or a combination thereof? What is the profile of the "typical" customer who frequents the center in terms of age, sex, ethnic background, income, and wealth? Is the typical customer a professional or a blue-collar worker? Doctors tend to locate in close proximity to hospitals. Supermarkets that focus on specific ethnic groups will be located in an area that has a high concentration of people of that ethnicity. At times, there is a synergistic relationship between tenants. If this exists, it should be identified and capitalized upon. For example, Walmart and Home Depot are anchors that generate huge amounts of traffic. Are there certain types of retailers, or better yet specific companies, that desire to be located in close proximity to these demand generators and are not objectionable to the demand generator? For example, as previously mentioned, food courts often work well in conjunction with entertainment facilities such as movie theaters. An imaging center complements orthopedic and neurological doctors' offices.

The Surrounding Area

It is also important to understand what is going on around the center. If the vacant lot across from the center will soon be a Super Walmart, how does that affect your marketing program? What if a shopping center is being demolished or renovated in close proximity to the subject property and the tenants from this center must find a new home? The soon-to-be-displaced tenants are a great source of leads.

> ### Rule Number 25
> Be aware of your surroundings and what is going on in the local market since that can have a dramatic impact on your marketing strategy and business success.

Practical Concerns: Temper the Marketing Plan with Market Knowledge

Let us assume that you have done your homework, and have analyzed the center's physical characteristics and its demand generators. Based upon these factors, you conclude that Trader Joe's would be an ideal tenant. The problem is that Trader Joe's already has a store across the street from the subject property! Your analysis must be tempered with market knowledge. The most important practical question often becomes: Based upon the size of the available space, what company is currently looking to rent space in this marketplace? The space might be ideal for Trader Joe's, but if Trader Joe's already has a presence in close proximity to the center in question, it is not likely to be a viable candidate for the vacancy, unless, of course, the prospect's lease is expiring and your location is far superior and would amount to an upgrade for this tenant. In contrast, let us say Smart and Final is attempting to get a foothold in this marketplace, yet does not currently have a store located nearby. It would jump to the front of your line. Smart and Final has an unfulfilled need that can be filled by your 20,000-square-feet anchor space. However, there are practical concerns, for example, there are two years to go on the Giant Green Grocer's lease. If Smart and Final is ready to go now, how do you deal with the lease expiration date? Will the Giant Green Grocer consider a payment by the landlord in return for terminating the lease? Given that the Giant Green Grocer is losing money, might not the tenant consider this course of action?

Leasing

In general, landlords seek long-term leases and tenants tend to want shorter terms with options to extend. Landlords want stability, which translates into a long-term commitment from the tenant, while tenants are not sure what will happen tomorrow and therefore usually attempt to limit their commitment while, if possible, keeping their future choices open-ended.

Strategy

The options to extend are a one-way street in the sense that they only benefit the tenant. If the option is favorable or at market, the tenant may extend. If the option is not favorable, the tenant is in no worse a position. He simply ignores the option and commences to negotiate an extension with the landlord. Options to extend are not bilateral, that is, they do not contain a provision that allows the landlord to require the tenant to extend the term of the lease. If the landlord commits significant monies toward improving the premises for the tenant then, logically, the landlord will insist on a term at least sufficient to recover the dollars spent—and probably significantly longer.

When leasing, a forward-thinking landlord will attempt to stagger lease maturities. A concentration of leases maturing in the same year can severely affect cash flow as well as impact capital outlays needed to retain the tenants. Also, an eye should be kept on the loan maturity. Lenders underwrite based upon leases in place. Therefore, a problem may arise if lease maturities and loan maturity converge. Similarly, lease negotiations should consider economic cycles. Landlords should attempt to anticipate down-cycles and set the lease maturity, if possible, past the projected weak market periods. In contrast, tenants, if possible, should attempt to renegotiate during a high-vacancy period. Obviously, it is difficult to predict the peaks and the valleys, but in a strong market, landlords can approach their tenants to renegotiate leases early and conversely, if the economy and specifically the subject building are suffering from a high vacancy rate, a tenant can then seek to extend the term of its lease.

Leasing In-House versus Employing an Outside

Broker

How you intend to market the property should be addressed. Will you market in-house or through a leasing broker? Does the owner have the time, ability, and inclination to attempt to lease-up the property? Does the owner have in-house personnel or specific leasing personnel that can take on this task? Does the owner want to control the beginning leasing effort, pick the "low-hanging fruit," and then turn the leasing efforts over to a professional? The problems with this policy are, first, that there usually is *no* low-hanging fruit and, second, the owner has to be careful that he does not take all of the juice out of whatever fruit there is, leaving nothing for the broker. In other words, the project can be whittled down to a size that makes it less than attractive, from an economic standpoint, to a quality leasing broker.

If you elect to hire a leasing broker, interview more than one company. Always ask who specifically is going to do what. Understand who ultimately is going to be in charge of the leasing assignment. At times, especially with large brokerage companies, you might meet with a senior leasing specialist who sells you on the company's capabilities but then you never see the same person again. The "grunts," that is, individuals with less experience, are assigned to do the tedious labor of working the market, making cold calls by knocking on doors and doing telephone solicitation. This might be an acceptable division of work, but you should at least understand what you are signing up for. An acceptable compromise might be to allow the less-experienced agents to do lead generation, but then require the more experienced broker to step in to coordinate the lease offer, lease negotiation, and lease closing. It is crucial to understand what you are getting for your money.

Exclusive versus Nonexclusive Authorization

An *exclusive authorization* says in effect that if, during an agreed time period, regardless of who procures the tenant, a lease is executed for the property, a commission is owed to the broker in whose favor the exclusive authorization runs. The language governing when a commission has been earned must be carefully scrutinized. Care must be taken to avoid a dispute with the listing broker. If the contract indicates a commission is owed when a willing and able tenant is found, a commission might be owed even if a lease is not consummated. Prudence might dictate that the contract indicate "no ticket, no laundry." In other words, only if a lease is entered into is a commission earned.

In contrast to an exclusive listing agreement, a *nonexclusive agreement* provides that if the broker brings in a tenant and a lease is consummated with that tenant, a commission is earned, but if another broker procures a tenant and a lease is finalized with the other broker's client, a commission is owed only to the procuring broker.

Most brokers require an exclusive authorization to induce them to work on a leasing assignment. They argue that they do not want to compete with the owner or expend efforts marketing a property when a potential prospect might learn about the project through their marketing efforts and then attempt to cut the broker out by going directly to the owner or using another agent.

Of course, parties can enter into variations and hybrid arrangements. For example, the broker might be paid a monthly fee and no additional commission upon lease consummation, or a monthly fee plus a reduced commission schedule on an exclusive or nonexclusive basis.

The Commission Amount

The commission schedule is always subject to negotiation. Typically, the leasing commission will be based on a standard within the local market. In some parts of the country, a fee based upon the square footage of the leased space, such as $6.00 per square foot, is typical. In other areas, a flat fee or a declining percentage such as the following might be the norm:

- 7 percent of the Base Rent for the first 12 months
- 6 percent of the Base Rent for the second 12 months
- 5 percent of the Base Rent for the third 12 months
- 4 percent of the Base Rent for the fourth 12 months
- 4 percent of the Base Rent for the fifth 12 months
- 3 percent of the Base Rent for the next 60 months
- 2 percent of the Base Rent for the balance of the term

The reasoning behind the declining percentage is threefold: (1) As the lease term is lengthened, the expectancy of collecting the rent is reduced and hence the brokerage fee should be reduced; (2) the absolute amount of the fee becomes sufficient to induce a broker to work the project and hence it need not increase further; and (3) the schedule reflects the market for this type of service.

When confronted with this type of a commission schedule, I will usually ask that the percentage be switched in the early years of the lease term. My argument is that I want to discourage short-term leases. My typical five-year leasing schedule reflects annual charges of 4 percent, 4 percent, 5 percent, 6 percent, and 7 percent in years one to five, respectively.

Another, and simpler, approach is to set the leasing commission at 4 to 6 percent flat for the first five years and then one-half of the agreed percentage thereafter.

If the commission is based upon a percentage of Base Rent, then defining what comprises Base Rent becomes important. By definition, Base Rent does not usually include any expense recovery by the landlord. Should there be a different leasing percentage for a gross lease as opposed to a net lease or a net, net lease, or a triple net lease? If you are calculating the commission using the Base Rent, then theoretically an adjustment should be made since, comparing apples to apples, the Base Rent in a gross lease will be higher than in a lease where the tenant is obligated to pay a portion of the operating expenses in addition to the Base Rent. An alternative way to adjust the commission between lease types would be to include all or a portion of the operating expenses within the definition of Base Rent for purposes of calculating the fee owed. Despite the potential disparity in the commission calculation between the lease types, usually the percentage is simply based upon the Base Rent with no adjustment for contractually charged and recoverable operating expenses.

Another issue that should be considered when entering into a leasing contract is the effect of free rent, or a tenant improvement allowance, or any other concession on the commission. If extensive concessions must be made, should the broker participate? Without adjustments, disparities may result. For example, if a tenant must be given a free build-out period and a free ramp-up period, and if the commission is based upon a percentage of the income generated, the commission is affected by the concessions. However, if the commission is based upon a dollar figure per square foot, the commission amount is unaffected by the concessions.

Should there be any adjustment in the commission schedule due to tenant improvement dollars above a certain standard level? The answer to this question depends both upon how the Base Rent was determined and on how the commission is calculated. The broker may argue that the commission should not be adjusted since the owner is receiving increased rent, that is, the "excess" tenant improvement allowance was factored into the rental rate. Therefore, if the compensation is based upon a flat fee or a rate per square foot, the owner should have no complaint since he is not paying more because of the enhanced rent. On the other hand, a commission based on a percentage of gross rent would increase the fee due to the overstandard tenant improvements. Usually the commission agreement is not adjusted to factor in build-out costs. It is usually considered just part of the deal.

Cobrokerage Arrangements

An area that is often not covered in a standard leasing authorization and one that should be clarified is how a commission will be shared, if at all, with a broker who is not related to the listing broker but who nevertheless procures a tenant. A typical arrangement is to increase the commission schedule by 1 percent for each category and agree to a 50/50 split of the fee. Usually, the broker representing the tenant seeks to achieve at least 4 percent for the first five years and 2 percent thereafter.

When Is the Commission Payable?

The agreement should also cover when the commission is payable. Brokers usually angle to receive payment in full when a lease is signed. The tenant has been identified, the lease has been drafted and negotiated, the lease has been executed, the job is done: Pay me. Owners, especially when the commission is large and/or when it is anticipated that the tenant will not be in place paying rent for a protracted period of time, usually seek to defer at least part of the fee. A fairly typical arrangement specifies that one-half of the commission is due and payable when the lease is executed and the other half is due and payable when the tenant moves into the suite and is paying rent. If an extensive free-rent period or a protracted build-out period is built into the lease, a compromise might be to set the payment for the second half of the commission at the earlier to occur of (1) a specified period such as three months from lease execution or (2) when the tenant is in place paying rent. In other words, set an outside date for the second half to be paid regardless of other delays. In an area that is experiencing high tenant delinquencies, the owner might attempt to have the commission schedule split into three payments with the last payment due after a seasoning period, that is, the tenant is current and in place for six months.

Exclusions from the Listing Agreement

Often, leasing efforts have been expended on projects before an authorization is agreed upon. The efforts might have been expended by the owner and/or by a broker that is different from the listing broker. This leads to the concept of "exclusions." The authorization to lease might exclude or carve out certain potential tenants from the listing agreement. Alternatively, as a compromise position, the agreement may provide that as to certain named prospects, the listing broker will be compensated at a reduced fee if a lease is consummated with these named parties.

The most common exclusion is for existing tenants. The owner reasons, "Why do I need a broker to negotiate with the tenants I already know? I am paying a broker a commission to find new prospects." This argument has some validity, provided the owner is active in the management of the project and has the ability to understand and negotiate the lease terms and conditions. The broker's counter, if applicable, might be that his potential fees are too small unless he can also work on renewals.

Lease Renewals and Extensions

A lease can be renewed on the same terms and conditions as it presently exists, or it can be renewed on different terms and conditions. Usually, at a minimum, when a lease is renewed, the base rent is altered. Similarly, the lease term can be extended without changing other provisions in the lease or, concurrent with the extension, the lease terms and conditions may be modified. For purposes of this section, a lease renewal shall be treated the same as a lease extension. A renewal or an extension shall be referred to interchangeably as a "renewal" or as an "extension."

If you elect to enter into an authorization to lease with a broker, it is important to specifically cover lease renewals. Lease renewals by definition relate to existing tenants and therefore, as previously stated, existing tenants may be excluded from the listing.

A distinction is sometimes made between renewals associated with tenants' leases procured during the authorization period versus renewals for tenants' leases entered into prior to the brokerage contract. The broker's argument is "I understand, Mr. Owner, your reasoning for excluding existing tenants since I did not bring them to the table; however, as to tenants I procured during the listing period, I should be covered for the lease they sign and paid on any renewal if those tenants renew their lease."

No distinction is usually made as to the documentation surrounding the renewal, that is, whether the tenant exercises an option to renew the lease or modifies an existing lease or negotiates a new lease. However, if the "renewal" is for other space within the project, it is probably technically not a renewal. The language in the contract controls.

- Management must decide whether or not it wants an outside leasing broker to negotiate with existing tenants. If the leasing assignment covers renewals, should the commission schedule be reduced given that identification of the prospect, arguably the most difficult aspect of the assignment, has been eliminated?
- Lease renewals include situations when a leasing broker procures a tenant during the authorization period, a lease is entered into, and when the lease expires the tenant extends the term of the lease by exercising an option to extend or possibly by entering into a new lease for the premises or entering into a new lease for another space within the project. Has a commission

been earned? The contract controls. There is no right answer. The broker has an argument that he procured the tenant. The owner may be concerned that the renewal probably will occur several years after the original lease was signed. When the lease is renewed, the owner may not have a relationship with the broker. In fact, the broker may no longer be in the leasing brokerage business!

Are Commissions Due upon Suite Expansions?

A similar issue to extensions revolves around expansions. Should the procuring broker be paid an additional fee if the tenant increases the suite size at a future date? What if the lease, when signed, posited that the suite would possibly be enlarged at a future date? There is no right answer to this question, but the important point is that this issue should be covered in the listing agreement.

Treatment of Commissions for the Month-to-Month Tenant

What if the tenant that is procured will not sign a long-term lease, but rather will only agree to a trial month-to-month tenancy until his business shows profitability. If the landlord is willing to give this tenant a try, how should the commission be structured? The problem is that the tenant, on 30-days' notice, may terminate the lease. On what basis do you set the commission amount? Usually, for month-to-month tenancies the payment is based upon a percentage of rent actually received. The commission is paid monthly as long as the tenant remains in occupancy paying rent.

Right of Offset

At times, the listing agreement may contain a provision that says, in essence, that if the landlord fails to pay the brokerage commission on or before its due date, then the broker may send a written notice to the landlord and the tenant of such failure, and if the landlord fails to pay the amount owing within 30 days after the notice, then the tenant shall be entitled to pay the broker directly the fee due and offset the amount paid to the broker against the tenant's next rental obligations coming due under the lease. The commission agreement language usually goes on to say that any amounts so offset from the tenant's rental obligations under the lease shall no longer be owed from the landlord to the broker and that this right of offset shall be set forth, in writing, within the lease document between landlord and the tenant.

In most cases, the landlord will strike this type of "self-help" provision, arguing that the broker has remedies built into the commission agreement if the landlord fails to pay its obligations, but that involving his tenants is not an appropriate remedy.

Implementation

Okay, you have analyzed the Center's characteristics, its existing tenant base, and its physical layout. You have determined what, if anything, is missing from the Center. You have developed a marketing game plan and hired a leasing broker. What is the next step?

What does the authorization say your broker is obligated to do? There may be a vague statement obligating the broker to use his best efforts to lease the property, but usually that is about it. The exclusive authorization is all about the broker getting paid; how much and when. The owner should include specific action items that the broker is mandated to perform, including preparing a leasing brochure, having weekly face-to-face or telephonic meetings, delivering monthly written reports, and generally following up on the marketing game plan.

Now we have analyzed the project and identified the potential type of tenants that would be a good fit. We may have actually identified specific tenants that would be good candidates for the vacant slots. We have also designed and produced a leasing brochure that highlights the project and provides potential tenant candidates with contact information. We have also created a written marketing game plan, part of which addresses implementation. It is now time to get out there and make the necessary contacts to implement the game plan.

What implementation boils down to is contacting the potential leasing candidates and following up with them. Contacting potential tenants should include all of the following:

- Making telephone calls.
- Sending mailers, including mailing out the leasing brochure.
- Knocking on the doors of the potential candidates.
- Canvassing the local area where the property is located.
- Contacting brokers, especially brokers that represent tenants.
- Creating a referral incentive program within your existing tenant base.
- Advertising.
- Making local community contacts, such as the local Chamber of Commerce.
- Placing "For Lease" signage on the project itself.

Rule Number 26

When attempting to lease-up your project, leave no stone unturned!

Leasing Brochure

Regardless of whether the property is to be marketed internally or through an outside broker, after a marketing game plan is generated, a leasing brochure should be produced. The objective of the brochure is to capture potential clients' attention without bogging them down with details at this point in time. Ideally, the brochure should be on an 8 ½" × 11" sheet of high-gloss paper. On the front, there might be a picture of the property and a listing of its salient features such as:

- Four-Story Medical Office Building
- Located on Campus of XYZ Hospital
- Convenient Freeway Accessibility
- Abundant parking—5 spaces per 1,000 net rentable square feet
- Suites ranging in size from 1,000 sq. feet to 20,000 sq. feet available
- Tenant Improvement package available

The reverse side of the brochure might feature a location map and contact information.

Leasing as an Art

Leasing is an art, not a science. It is crucial to be able to screen a potential tenant not only for financial strength and credit, but also with regard to their moral fiber and potential strengths. Are they likely capable of making a go of it in the face of obstacles? Since there are always trials and tribulations when running a business, the tenant's commitment to the business is an important ingredient. It is also important to have a vision of what works for your property. Often tenant compatibility and, ideally, synergy is a key to the long-term viability of a property.

Before you turn your broker loose to find prospects to fill the vacancies, note that there are several traps and pitfalls that should be avoided. A few of them are outlined next.

Exclusivity Provisions

How do you react if the shopping center has a beauty salon and your leasing agent calls saying he has another beauty salon prospect? What issues does this raise? The question arises: Does the lease with an existing tenant contain an exclusivity provision barring other tenants from this type of competing usage? In other words, has the existing tenant been given the exclusive right to sell this type of product or render this type of service? This issue is a threshold question and must be examined at the outset, not only in conjunction with a specific potential tenant but also with the leasing agent, who should be informed from the get-go what kinds of vendors may not be solicited because an existing tenant has the sole right to sell certain products or render certain services.

Even if there is no contractual prohibition from renting to another tenant who intends to sell or render a similar product or service, it is still wise to ask if it is a good business policy to have two or more competing firms in the same center selling similar goods and services. The answer to this question revolves around several factors, including the size of the center, the size of the general market, and whether or not the tenants are direct competitors or, essentially, serve different market niches. It is important to have a vision as to how the tenants might work together for the overall benefit of the property and, ideally, this concept should be conveyed to the leasing broker.

Restrictive Covenants

Exclusive-use provisions may be found in existing leases as mentioned above. In addition, a lease may contain a restrictive covenant that prohibits other tenants from coming into the center and doing business in a manner barred by the provision, whether or not the existing tenant is selling the prohibited commodity or service. Restrictions may be found in existing tenant leases, such as when a supermarket or other major tenant negotiates a provision blocking other tenants from selling similar or competitive goods in the center. The covenant might also restrict a type of usage that it deems harmful to its business. For example, an investment firm might desire to prohibit a bar or pub from being located within a short distance from their site. They might want this restriction because they feel a bar or pub will detract from the professional nature of their business.

Restrictive covenants may also be located in other documents affecting the project. As previously mentioned, the most common additional place the lease restrictions may be found are in CC&Rs or in ground-lease provisions. For example, assume a medical office building is located on ground-leased property on a hospital campus. The lessor of the land is the hospital. Wanting to control the competitive usage in the immediate area that surrounds its premises, the hospital uses the ground-lease to bar physical therapy, out-patient surgery, and radiology including X-ray, CAT scan, and MRI services in the medical office building.

> ## Rule Number 27
> Make sure you understand what types of tenants are permitted tenants before you start the search for new tenants and certainly before you execute a lease.

Interference with Tenant's Business

Let us assume you own a shopping center. One of the tenants is a beauty salon, La Salon, owned by Jacques LeBeau. The beauty salon is having financial difficulties. It is three months delinquent in its rental obligation. The owner has been trying to sell his business for several months and advises you that he is in negotiations with a potential buyer, Joe Purchaser. LeBeau introduces you to Joe Purchaser during a conference call. The sale falls through and you evict La Salon due to its failure to pay the rental obligations. One month later, Joe Purchaser approaches you to rent the space formerly occupied by La Salon. You enter into a new five-year lease with Joe Purchaser, who renovates the space and opens a new beauty salon. The next day, La Salon's owner serves you with a complaint claiming, among other things, that you conspired with Joe Purchaser to deprive him from the profit from the sale of his business to Joe and interfered with his business relationships.

The facts are that you had empty space, the LeBeau sale to Joe Purchaser had fallen through, the Purchaser approached you, and in fact you have a duty to mitigate damages and lease the beauty salon space to reduce LeBeau's damages. To avoid an interference with contractual relations and/or a conspiracy type of a claim, you might obtain an authorization from LeBeau that allows you to enter into a new lease with Purchaser and/or obtain an indemnity from Purchaser protecting you from claims by LeBeau. Additionally, after the LeBeau/Purchaser sale falls apart and when Purchaser approaches you about a new lease, you might send a letter to LeBeau advising him that you are attempting to mitigate damages and that Joe Purchaser has approached you and you are therefore entering into negotiations with Purchaser for a new lease. This is a gray area and, therefore, prudence and caution are advised.

Rule Number 28

When considering entering into a lease, be cautious when dealing with parties who were previously under contract to purchase a business within the center.

The Screening Process

Okay, we have our written marketing plan, we have hired a broker, and, through the broker's marketing efforts, a prospective tenant has appeared. What is the next step?

It must be determined if the applicant meets the owner's financial and credit standards to warrant entering into a lease. To some extent, this test becomes a market issue. If the economy and the center are doing great and the owner has choices, he can be selective and discriminating. However, if times are tough and the center is experiencing significant vacancy, the owner's options are less abundant. It is nonetheless important to have a minimum standard, especially if the owner must spend money to put the tenant in place.

What documentation should the owner seek in order to qualify the prospect? Typical materials include a rental application, which should contain an authorization to run a credit report, a resume or a short narrative biographical sketch, financial data such as annual income and expenses, a balance sheet, and tax returns. As previously noted, leasing is an art, not a science. Therefore, it is essential that the landlord and/or the landlord's representative have a face-to-face meeting with the prospective tenant.

What is your reaction if your broker advises that he has found a well-qualified prospective tenant and when you call the prospect the first thing he says is "What rent per square foot are you charging?" Potential lease candidates also often go through a screening process of the prospective premises and possibly the landlord. Usually, what the prospective tenant is saying really is, "Tell me what your lease rate is so I can eliminate you from my list of potential space candidates." The tenant is trying to screen the landlord's space and narrow his search for a deal.

When asked this question, I invariably answer the question with a question. How long a lease are you willing to commit to? I often do not get an unequivocal response and therefore can easily say, "How can I quote you a definitive rent per square foot number when you can not tell me how long you will lease the space for? The rate for a 10-year lease is different from the rate for a five-year lease." At times the response is, "Okay, let's assume the lease term is five years." My next question stops them cold. I ask, "What kind of a tenant improvement allowance do you want?" The response usually is "How do I know? I haven't seen the space yet so I don't know what is needed." I respond, "Exactly. You don't even know if you like the suite and I certainly do not know what, if any, remodeling you will require or the cost associated with it . . . so how can I quote a rate per square foot?" The point is that if you truly have a potential lease candidate, in order to move the process forward, you must get him involved in the process and excited about the suite. You must at a minimum show him the space. Answering the question "What do you charge per square foot?" usually results in a lost prospect.

> ## Rule Number 29
> If the first question a prospective tenant asks is how much you charge—What is the rent per square foot?—don't answer the question.

If the owner feels comfortable with the prospect, the terms and conditions of the lease must be negotiated. This process can be done verbally and thereafter a lease can be drawn, but it is more common to present a written letter of intent to the prospect, from which the discussions may commence.

Letter of Intent

In order to properly draft a letter of intent (LOI), it is important to be familiar with the property and, more specifically, with what market rent is and what you have been able to achieve at the Center. A review of the current rent roll is helpful. Please refer to the Crossroads Plaza Rent Roll found in Exhibit A.8 on the companion website. A perusal of Exhibit A.8 reveals that the lease rates are very erratic, with the range going from $.49 per square foot per month for the large 205,000-square-foot supermarket to $1.70 per square foot for the 5,000-square-foot restaurant/tavern. The most recent lease for 1,200 square feet was cut at $1.08 per square foot per month on a triple net basis. The vacant space is shown at a scheduled rent of $1.17 per square foot per month. Before the LOI is issued, you should be familiar with any usage or other restrictions applicable to the project. A review of the Project Summary Sheet, discussed below, might clarify these concerns. To speed up the process, you might also have prepared a standard letter of intent and a standard lease. Of course, the standard form must be tailored for the specific lease transaction, but the standard form is a good starting point. A letter of intent is often used as an expedient way to "cut a deal," that is, to get directly to the salient business points without the clutter of all of the other lease provisions.

A sample letter of intent covering the key business might look as follows:

Landlord	EC California Gold, LLC.
Tenant	The Hobby Shop, Inc.
Guarantor	Peter Smith and Mary Smith.
Premises	Suite 101 consisting of approximately 2,600 net rentable square feet.
Building	A 120,000 net rentable square foot Shopping Center plus all associated common areas including the surface parking.
Term	Five years commencing January 1, 2009.
Rent	The monthly Base Rent to be Three Thousand Five Hundred Ten Dollars ($3,510.00).
Rent Adjustments	The Base Rent to increase annually by four percent (4%).
Lease Type	Triple Net. Tenant to pay its pro rata share of operating expenses.
Tenant's Maintenance Obligations	Tenant shall be responsible to maintain in good condition the interior of the Premises and shall be obligated for the maintenance, repair, and upkeep of the HVAC unit solely serving the Premises. Tenant shall also be responsible to keep in full force and effect a full service contract for the HVAC unit from a HVAC company approved by Landlord, approval not to be unreasonably withheld, delayed, or conditioned.
Tenant Improvement Allowance	Landlord to disburse Twenty-Five Thousand Dollars ($25,000.00) to Tenant for use on approved Tenant Improvements upon receipt of:
	1. Description of the work done and/or materials installed.
	2. Copy of applicable invoices.
	3. Copy of payment check to vendor or contractor.
	4. Unconditional notarized lien release.

Security Deposit	One month's Base Rent.
Building Hours	Tenant shall have access to the Premises 24/7.
Confidentiality	Tenant shall not disclose the Lease terms contained herein to any third party, except Tenant's accountant or attorney-at-law or as otherwise approved by Landlord.

This Letter of Intent shall not be binding upon the parties and is merely an expression of interest. Only if Landlord and Tenant execute a lease shall there be a binding contractual relationship between the parties.

The following is a brief commentary on the above letter of intent combined with a hypothetical negotiation between the landlord, Miles Mission, and the prospective tenant, Peter Smith. The emphasis is placed upon shedding additional light on the leasing issues and especially on business areas and deal points that should be reflected upon as the transaction is negotiated.

An accurate recitation of the parties is important. The landlord should understand clearly who the obligor on the lease will be. If the obligor is a married man or woman, consideration should be had on whether both parties should sign the lease. This avoids a finger-pointing argument in the event of a default. If the husband is obligated on the lease and the landlord seeks to collect delinquent rent, the landlord wants to avoid the husband's argument that "I own nothing; everything is in my wife's name."

If multiple tenants comprise the obligor, the LOI should recite that they shall be jointly and severally liable. Joint and several liability results in all of the signors responsible for the rent ("joint") and each signor individually responsible for the entire rent ("severally"). When the landlord requires joint and several liability, one obligor cannot say, "Here is my one-eighth of the rent, collect the balance of the rent from the other seven obligors." Of course, the tenants should have an agreement between themselves allocating, among other things, the monthly rent obligation.

Often, a tenant will request the ability to sign the lease in the name of his business entity. They usually argue that by doing so the rent will be an expense within the partnership, corporation, limited liability company, and so forth. Of course, if the prospective tenant is Microsoft, no problem. The reality is that 99 percent of prospective tenants are not "credit" tenants and the desire to move to an entity obligor insulates their liability. The landlord's counter to this proposal, although not without its own set of risks, is to require a personal guaranty. If a guaranty is required, it is prudent to include such language in the LOI and, again, if the guarantor is married, both the husband and wife should execute the guaranty.

A letter of intent is a lease proposal. The letter of intent is usually stated as nonbinding as stated earlier; however, alternative language might indicate "This Letter of Intent shall be binding upon the parties and confirmed in a lease to be executed by Landlord and Tenant." Although this provision suggests that the LOI is binding and enforceable against both landlord and tenant, in actuality it probably is not binding due to its lack of definiteness. There are too many areas not covered in the LOI, and even the covered areas usually are set forth in general terms.

In our hypothetical scenario, Peter Smith, after reviewing the LOI, admits to Mission that his business is a start-up, but he argues that he has a lot of experience in the hobby field, having worked for several other hobby shops over the past 15 years. He also indicates that he is not willing to guaranty the lease. He argues that he is putting all the money he has, not to mention his heart and soul, into this business. He also states that, given the economic climate, a severe recession, with businesses going under left and right and unemployment approaching 10 percent, that the proposed $1.35 per square foot per month rent is too high, that the annual escalation of four percent makes no sense in a deflationary economy, and that the tenant improvement allowance of $25,000, which equates to $10 per square foot, does not work since the build-out will cost approximately $87,500, which equates to $35 per square foot.

Miles reasons that he needs tenants, given his occupancy, and after meeting with Peter he feels confident that Peter will give the business his total commitment. However, Miles is firm that the $1.35 per square foot per month is at or below market price and that he wants Peter to have his own money in the transaction to assure his attention. Miles proposes to give up the guaranty by significantly increasing the security deposit. He also decides to ameliorate the rent issue by offering some free rent. Miles understands Peter's concern about the build-out cost and agrees to increase the tenant improvement allowance, yet feels the increased allowance should come at a cost. He therefore agrees to increase the tenant improvement allowance by $25,000, with the stipulation that a cost to the funds be attributed and amortized into the rent. Miles asserts that his cost of capital is 8 percent, so using his financial calculator he figures that the additional charge should be $387 per month if spread over a seven-year lease. Miles realizes that this modification might run counter to ameliorating the rent, but he feels that that is a fair trade-off if Peter desires that Miles fund additional tenant improvement costs. Again, Miles' biggest concern is having Peter financially committed in terms of hard cash invested. Miles figures that under this structure, Peter will have, at the least, approximately $60,900 of cash at stake going into the transaction: $37,500 in tenant improvement money and a $23,400 security deposit. Miles wants to cover the potential inflation factor and he is not set on the fixed annual bump, so he decides to give Peter options. Miles modifies the LOI as follows:

Landlord	EC California Gold, LLC.
Tenant	The Hobby Shop, Inc.
Premises	Suite 101 consisting of approximately 2,500 net rentable square feet
Building	A 120,000 net rentable square foot Shopping Center plus all associated common areas including the surface parking.
Term	Seven years commencing January 1, 2009.
Rent	The monthly Base Rent to be Three Thousand Nine Hundred Dollars ($3,900.00).
Free Rent	Tenant shall pay one-half of the Base Rent for months one through six of the Term.
Rent Adjustments	The Base Rent to increase annually by (1) Four Percent (4%) or (2) CPI with a floor of 3% and a ceiling of 5% or (3) CPI. Tenant to select choice 1, 2, or 3 prior to lease execution. Choice selected shall be for entire Lease Term.
Lease Type	Triple Net. Tenant to pay its pro rata share of operating expenses.
Tenant's Maintenance Obligations	Tenant shall be responsible to maintain in good condition the interior of the Premises and shall be obligated for the maintenance, repair, and upkeep of the HVAC unit solely serving the Premises. Tenant shall also be responsible to keep in full force and effect a full service contract for the HVAC unit from a HVAC company approved by Landlord, approval not to be unreasonably withheld, or conditioned, or delayed.
Tenant Improvement Allowance	Landlord to disburse Fifty Thousand Dollars ($50,000.00) to Tenant for use on approved Tenant Improvements upon receipt of:
	1. Description of the work done and/or materials installed.
	2. Copy of applicable invoices.
	3. Copy of payment check to vendor or contractor.
	4. Unconditional notarized lien release.
Security Deposit	Six month's Base Rent, that is, $23,400.00
Building Hours	Tenant shall have access to the Premises 24/7.
Confidentiality	Tenant shall not disclose the Lease terms contained herein to any third party, except Tenant's accountant or attorney-at-law or as otherwise approved by Landlord.

After Peter reviews the LOI, he calls Miles and indicates that the parties are getting closer to a deal, but he is concerned about five issues:

1. Miles had set the lease commencement as of January 1, 2009. Peter points out that it is now November 20, 2008. Peter argues that there is no way he can have the tenant improvements built-out prior to year-end with the holidays coming up and, in fact, he has not even applied for a permit.

2. Peter expresses his concern that he does not have a handle on the triple net expenses. He requests that Miles cap this cost and that increases in real estate taxes due to a sale be excluded from the triple net charges.

3. Peter is willing to take on the repair and maintenance obligation of the

HVAC unit, but he questions its current condition. He wants to make sure, going in, that it is in good working condition, and if it needs to be replaced that that would be a capital expense, an obligation of the Landlord.

4. Peter says he is unclear how the tenant improvement allowance works. Does he have to spend money and then get reimbursed, or can he just give Miles a copy of the invoice for services or materials?

5. Peter indicates that his goal is to build up a business and, that if it is successful, the location will be crucial since his customers will be used to going to this location. He therefore asks for two five-year options to renew.

Addressing some of Peter's concerns, Miles revises the LOI as follows:

Landlord	EC California Gold, LLC.
Tenant	The Hobby Shop, Inc.
Premises	Suite 101 consisting of approximately 2,500 net rentable square feet.
Building	A 120,000 net rentable square foot Shopping Center plus all associated common areas including the surface parking.
Term	Seven years commencing upon Lease execution ("Commencement Date").
Rent	The monthly Base Rent to be Three Thousand Seven Hundred Sixty-Two Dollars ($3,762.00).
Rent Commencement Date	Tenant's obligation to pay the Base Rent shall commence upon the earlier to occur of substantial completion of the tenant improvements or April 1, 2009. Tenant shall pay only one-half of the Base Rent for the first six months after the Rent Commencement Date.
Rent Adjustments	The Base Rent to increase annually by (1) Four Percent (4%) or (2) CPI with a floor of 3% and a ceiling of 5% or (3) CPI. Tenant to select choice 1, 2, or 3 prior to lease execution. Choice selected shall be for entire Lease Term.
Lease Type	Triple Net. Tenant to pay its pro rata share of operating expenses. However, Tenant's pro rata share of operating expenses for the first two years of the Lease Term will not exceed $.40 per square foot per month.
HVAC and Maintenance of the Premises	Landlord agrees to have the HVAC unit for the Premises serviced and in good working condition prior to the Rent Commencement Date. Tenant shall be responsible to maintain in good condition the interior of the Premises and shall be obligated for the maintenance, repair, and upkeep of the HVAC unit solely serving the Premises. Tenant shall also be responsible to keep in full force and effect a full-service contract for the HVAC unit from a HVAC company approved by Landlord, approval not to be unreasonably withheld, or conditioned, or delayed. Landlord agrees, at Landlord's sole cost and expense, to replace the HVAC unit in the event the HVAC unit's condition, at any time during the Term, requires replacement.
Tenant Improvement Allowance	Tenant to pay for the first Thirty-Seven Thousand Five Hundred Dollars ($37,500) of tenant improvements. Payments to be verified by a copy of the applicable contract, cancelled checks, and appropriate releases. Landlord to disburse the next Fifty Thousand Dollars ($50,000.00) to Tenant for use on approved tenant improvements upon receipt of:
	1. Description of the work done and/or materials installed.
	2. Copy of applicable invoices.
	3. Unconditional notarized lien release.
	Tenant shall bear the cost of any tenant improvement expense in excess of $87,500.
Security Deposit	Six month's Base Rent, i.e., $22,572.00
Building Hours	Tenant shall have access to the Premises 24/7.
Options to Renew	Provided there is no default under the Lease,
	Tenant shall have two five-year options to renew the Lease on the same terms and conditions, except this option provision, the tenant improvement allowance, and the free rent shall not apply and the Base Rent and annual escalations shall equal the fair rental value and annual increases as determined by Landlord, in Landlord's sole discretion

Confidentiality	Tenant shall not disclose the Lease terms contained herein to any third party, except Tenant's accountant or attorney-at-law or as otherwise approved by Landlord.

Miles has agreed to give Peter sufficient time to build-out the improvements, but wants to ensure that his feet are to the fire, so he inserts an outside date when Base Rent starts in any event. Miles makes a distinction between the Commencement Date and the Rent Commencement Date. His intention is to make sure the lease starts when Peter is given possession. He wants to make sure all of the lease provisions, including the insurance requirements, are in full force and effect during the tenant improvement build-out period. This is accomplished by having the lease effective at execution.

Although Miles is willing to compromise on the triple net charges and put a cap on the charges for the first two years, he is unwilling to eliminate real property tax increases due to a sale. Miles reasons that he knows the cost of running the center now and that that cost has been fairly stable at $.35 to $.40 per square foot per month. Therefore, he feels that that cost will not get away from him if he caps it at $.40 per square foot per month. He reasons that going out more than two years is too risky, and that although he currently has no intention of selling the property, "you never know"; if he eliminates the increase in real property taxes that could directly affect the sales price. In California, the buyer might correctly argue that real property taxes on sale will adjust to market, that given this exception, the increase in taxes could not, to the extent of the tenant's share, be passed on; the NOI would decrease and therefore the value would be reduced.

Miles considers Peter's comments regarding the HVAC unit valid. He knows the unit is in working condition because the prior tenant who just moved out had no complaints, but having the unit serviced, the filters changed, and so on is probably a good idea. Miles does not mind putting in the LOI his obligation to replace the unit as necessary. This provision was going to be documented in the lease in any event.

Miles attempts to clarify how the tenant improvement allowance will work. He wants to make sure that there are sufficient monies to complete the build-out, so he requires that Peter put his contribution in first. Once that is done, he feels that he is willing to put in the next $50,000, his obligation, not as a reimbursement but rather as a direct payment. He keeps the payments going to Peter, not a contractor, since he wants Peter to be satisfied with the work and responsible for monitoring the improvements.

The options to renew only inure to the benefit of the tenant. Nonetheless,

Miles is willing to grant the options because he reasons he wants a tenant in place and, as long as Peter is current, not in default, he may as well work with Peter as opposed to a new party. Miles also proposed an option in which he feels he has all of the control. The rent is to be set at market in his discretion, and there are no other concessions such as free rent or tenant improvement monies.

After reviewing the revised LOI, Peter tells Miles he is in agreement with the overall concepts, but he feels the option language should be more balanced, so that if he does not agree with the Landlord's estimate of the fair rental amount there should be a procedure to set the rate. Also, he mentions that one of the key reasons he is going into this shopping center is because of the potential traffic from the supermarket. He has heard that the anchor tenant is not doing well and has only a short time on its lease. He therefore proposes a cotenancy clause that will provide that if the Giant Green Grocer or a comparable supermarket does not occupy the main anchor space for a six-month period, that The Hobby Shop may terminate its lease.

Miles' response is that he is willing to insert an objective standard to set the rate for the options if the tenant feels that the rate the landlord comes up with exceeds market, but he declines to include a cotenancy provision. Miles indicates to Peter that The Hobby Shop must stand on its own two feet; he cannot control what another tenant will or will not do. Also, if the Giant Green Grocer does not renew, he might put in a discount store that could be as beneficial to The Hobby Store as the supermarket. Finally, he states that this type of an issue is a business risk that The Hobby Store must bear, especially in light of Miles' investment of $50,000 into The Hobby Store's tenant improvements and the free rent granted. Miles reissues the LOI as shown below, which is signed by both Landlord and Tenant.

Landlord	EC California Gold, LLC.
Tenant	The Hobby Shop, Inc.
Premises	Suite 101 consisting of approximately 2,500 net rentable square feet.
Building	A 120,000 net rentable square foot Shopping Center plus all associated common areas including the surface parking.
Term	Seven years commencing upon Lease execution ("Commencement Date")
Base Rent	The monthly Base Rent to be Three Thousand Seven Hundred Sixty-Two Dollars ($3,762.00).
Rent Commencement Date	Tenant's obligation to pay the Base Rent shall commence upon the earlier to occur of substantial completion of the tenant improvements or April 1, 2009. Tenant shall pay only one-half of the Base Rent for the first six months after the Rent Commencement Date.
Rent Adjustments	The Base Rent to increase annually by (1) Four Percent (4%) or (2) CPI with a floor of 3% and a ceiling of 5% or (3) CPI. Tenant to select choice 1, 2, or 3 prior to lease execution. Choice selected shall be for entire Lease Term.
Lease Type	Triple Net. Tenant to pay its pro rata share of operating expenses. However, Tenant's pro rata share of operating expenses for the first two years of the Lease Term will not exceed $.40 per square foot per month.

HVAC and Maintenance of the Premises	Landlord agrees to have the HVAC unit for the Premises serviced and in good working condition prior to the Rent Commencement Date. Tenant shall be responsible to maintain in good condition the interior of the Premises and shall be obligated for the maintenance, repair, and upkeep of the HVAC unit solely serving the Premises. Tenant shall also be responsible to keep in full force and affect a full-service contract for the HVAC unit from a HVAC company approved by Landlord, approval not to be unreasonably withheld, or conditioned, or delayed. Landlord agrees, at Landlord's sole cost and expense, to replace the HVAC unit in the event the HVAC unit's condition, at any time during the Term, requires replacement.
Tenant Improvement Allowance	Tenant to pay for the first Thirty-Seven Thousand Five Hundred Dollars ($37,500) of tenant improvements. Payments to be verified by a copy of the applicable contract, cancelled checks, and appropriate lien releases. Landlord to disburse the next Fifty Thousand Dollars ($50,000.00) to Tenant for use on approved tenant improvements upon receipt of:
	1. Description of the work done and/or materials installed.
	2. Copy of applicable invoices.
	3. Unconditional notarized lien release.
	Tenant shall bear the cost of any tenant improvement expense in excess of $87,500.
Security Deposit	Six month's Base Rent, that is, $22,572.00
Building Hours	Tenant shall have access to the Premises 24/7.
Options to Renew	Provided there is no default under the Lease, Tenant shall have two five-year options to renew the Lease on the same terms and conditions, except this option provision, the tenant improvement allowance, and the free rent shall not apply and the Base Rent and annual escalations shall equal the fair rental value and annual increase as determined by Landlord, in Landlord's sole discretion. In the event Tenant disagrees with Landlord's determination of fair rental value, an arbitration procedure to determine Base Rent and annual escalations shall be set forth in the Lease.
Confidentiality	Tenant shall not disclose the Lease terms contained herein to any third party, except Tenant's accountant or attorney-at-law or as otherwise approved by Landlord.

Comparison of Lease Terms

The prior discussion about the LOI is illustrative of the give-and-take negotiation that results in the final lease. The problem is that it lacks a method to quantitatively compare alternative lease proposals. Yes, some of the negotiated terms do not involve the purely economic provisions, but to the extent the monetary deal points are being traded, it is important to set up a model so that the give-and-take is better understood.

In grade school we are given problems such as, Is $3/5$ less than, equal to, or greater than $14/25$? In order to make this determination a common denominator is found and both fractions are converted to a fraction with the same denominator. In our example, 25 is the lowest common denominator. Converting both fractions to a denominator of 25 results in $3/5 = 15/25$ and $14/25$. Clearly therefore $3/5$ is greater than $14/25$.

How does a landlord determine if the lease terms are a reasonable package to offer? How can a tenant assess the options? Why not build in six months of free rent rather than three months? If you increase the tenant improvement allowance and reduce the free rent on a quantitative basis, how does that affect the landlord's return? Is there a methodology to compare variations in offered terms to assess the relative value of an offer?

Let us assume that you have just acquired a project. Let us also assume that during the process of the acquisition you made certain assumptions on what you felt were achievable goals in terms of lease-up parameters and eventual sale. Your assumptions were that during a five-year holding period, your initial rent would $3.00 per square foot per month, escalating 3 percent per year. Furthermore, you assumed that it would take nine months to lease-up the vacant space with a concession package of a 3 percent paid for leasing commissions and a $35 per square foot tenant improvement allowance. Also, you assumed that at the end of five years you would sell the building at a 7.75 percent cap rate with a cost of sale of 4 percent.

Along comes a prospect who says he wants minimal fix-up costs and as low a rent as possible. You think of offering $2.75 per square foot per month, increasing 3 percent per year, with a concession package of half Base Rents for one year and a tenant improvement allowance of $2.50 per square foot, which is what you have estimated will be the cost to paint the premises.

From a present value standpoint, is the proposal you are thinking of offering less than, equal to, or greater than the standard you set up when purchasing the property? Exhibit 10.1 is a simple Argus analysis showing that the proposal is better than the standard set-up during due diligence. The upper portion of the chart shows target or standard lease terms and conditions. In this case, it assumes an initial annual rent of $36 per square foot, increasing 3 percent per year. A value is calculated in the fifth year based upon reasonable assumptions. The rent concessions reduce income. The result is a cash-flow stream that can be reduced to a present value at an assumed discount rate. The bottom portion of the chart inserts proposed lease terms. The present value is again determined. The present value of the standard can then be compared to the present value of the proposed lease terms to derive a comparison of how the proposal stacks up to the target illustration. If the present value of the proposed lease terms exceeds the standard, then perhaps the landlord should move forward with the transaction. If the present value of the proposed lease terms is less than the standard, then perhaps the offer should be modified.

Exhibit 10.1 Lease Terms Comparison Analysis

	Year				
	1	2	3	4	5
Projected income	$36.00	$37.08	$38.19	$39.34	$40.52
Sale value of income @ 7.75 cap with 4 percent cost of sale					$501.90
Leasing commission (3%)	(27.00)				
Downtime 9 months	(35.00)				
Tenant improvements	(35.00)				
Cost analysis	$(61.00)	$37.08	$38.19	$39.34	$542.42
Return					
Present value at 8.77%	$389.32				
Leasing Proposal					
Rent	33.00	33.99	35.01	36.06	37.14
Sale value of income @ 7.75 cap with 4% cost of sale					$460.08
Free rent (6 months)	(16.50)				
Tenant improvements	(4.00)				
Cost analysis	$12.50	$33.99	$35.01	$36.06	$497.22
Present value at 8.77%	$419.78				

This type of analysis is a rational method to compare alternative deal structures. All too often, real estate professionals make economic decisions based on emotional factors rather than based upon a reasoned, economic model.

Lease Administration

A system should be created to move from lease execution through monthly rental billing.

In our organization, the office manager, within a short time frame after a lease is consummated, scans the lease into the computer and creates a permanent lease file. As an additional precautionary measure, it is prudent to store a copy of the scanned file offsite, for example, with counsel. The property manager for the applicable property then completes a lease abstract. A copy of the lease and the lease abstract is then given to accounting, which inputs the basic rental terms into the computer so that monthly invoices can be generated and a rent history established.

Lease Abstract

As mentioned above, a lease abstract should be created shortly after the lease has been entered into. The lease abstract attempts to summarize the key terms and conditions of the lease. Obvious items such as the base rent schedule should be outlined. In addition, it is helpful to highlight unusual provisions such as rights of first refusal, any termination rights, or the right to reduce the size of the suite upon the occurrence of certain events, and so on. Like the Lease Summary Binder, the lease abstract should be a document that is a useful living tool so that as other information about the tenant is learned, the abstract can be annotated with additional information. For example, often at the outset of the lease relationship, it may not be clear who the main tenant contact will be. However, as time passes, a working relationship develops and the contact person then can be listed in the abstract with his or her office number, a cell-phone number, and an e-mail address. As another example, let us assume the tenant goes into occupancy and six months later installs a security system. The lease abstract might be a convenient place to document the security code to be used in emergencies or to otherwise gain access to the tenant's premises.

Management

Organization, execution, and follow-up are the key factors in property management. Each property should be viewed as an independent business, as its own profit center.

The management of a project is the overall running of the asset. It can be divided into four segments: planning, implementing, monitoring, and reporting.

Planning

Planning is also discussed in Chapter 1. A written business plan as well as goals, property-by-property action items, and priority lists should be composed. Please refer back to Chapter 1 (including Exhibit 1.1).

An annual budget for each property is essential. The process of budgeting forces you to review your cash flow, your capital reserves, and problem areas in each property. Part of the budgeting process is to compare what was spent last year with what was spent during the current year and what is anticipated will be spent next year on each line item. By doing this, those items that are out of line, the variances, are highlighted and can be discussed.

Additionally, if your portfolio contains several similar properties, comparisons can be made between the properties to attempt to discern standout variances. The comparison is facilitated by translating the income and expenses into a per-square-foot number. Care must be taken to compare apples to apples since different geographic areas can have significantly differing factors that might affect the analysis. For example, the extremely hot summer temperature in Palm Springs, Las Vegas, and Phoenix increase the cost of roof replacement, parking lot repaving, and HVAC repairs as compared to those structures in a more temperate climate such as Los Angeles.

The budgeting process is geared to focusing on where the funds for the project will be spent during the coming year. Therefore, important areas to discuss include what leases are maturing and the present condition of those suites as well as what capital improvements, such as painting, paving, or roof replacement, will be needed over the next calendar year. Given the nature of capital improvements, major cash outlays, the budgeting process for these items may extend over several years. Ideally, bids for the needed capital improvements should be secured prior to budget discussions. Without knowing the associated cost, it is difficult to make informed decisions about where to spend limited resources.

Rule Number 30

Pricing is needed in order to make informed management decisions.

Implementing

To some extent, implementing is a function of the size of one's organization. If you have a small shop with one or two individuals, guess who takes out the garbage? Small to medium-size real estate companies outsource more functions than larger companies, which have the internal staff to take care of a greater range of matters.

Once a new property is acquired, the first step is an accounting function to set up the books. A balance sheet, income and expense analysis, and bank account information must be input into the computer. Computer programs such as Yardi and QuickBooks Pro have software designed to assist this process. The key data relating to each lease must also be inputed. The lease abstract can assist as a double-check, but the actual signed lease should be used for the data assembly. The computer program will pick up changes in monthly rent, so for billing purposes this aspect of the process becomes automated.

The computer facilitates issuance of monthly bills and receipts. When the rent checks come in for payment, the payment must be posted and a rent history is thereby created.

When a rent check is received, should it be posted to the most delinquent item or the current month's outstanding debt? The general accounting rule is last in, first out. Meaning that the last payment you receive gets applied to the most delinquent item. Notwithstanding this accounting rule, the lease controls. Most leases state: "All payments received by Landlord from Tenant shall be applied to the oldest payment obligation owed by Tenant to Landlord."

In California, by Code, you may go back only one year to determine the delinquent amount for purposes of the three-day notice to pay or quit and the unlawful detainer, that is, the lawsuit to evict a tenant. If the tenant cures the delinquency within the three-day period for the amount owed, then he may not be evicted. Nonetheless, the tenant still owes the outstanding balance beyond the one-year period and the landlord may file a lawsuit to collect the amount owed.

The manager's role vis-à-vis the property, as stated earlier, is a function of the size of the company as well as the type of leases involved. In other words, management should take the time to understand what responsibilities rest with the tenant and what responsibilities must be borne by the landlord. Full-service gross leases place more burdens on the landlord while, in contrast, bond leases pass the obligations for the care of the premises and the project to the tenant.

Management personnel should take the time and effort to read the applicable leases, so a clear understanding of the delineation of responsibilities is made.

Notwithstanding the general rule that the language in the lease controls, there are gray areas that must be dealt with on a fairness basis. For example, if a plumbing backup occurs in the tenant's bathroom, is the cost the tenant's expense or the landlord's expense? The determining factor is usually where the blockage occurred. If it is localized in the bathroom toilet, the expense should be covered by the tenant. However, if the stoppage is in a main sewer line far removed from the tenant's shop, it is the landlord's expense. As a practical matter, it is often difficult to determine where the blockage occurred and for sake of tenant relations the landlord usually picks up the repair cost.

A light goes out in the tenant's suite. Who is responsible for replacing the bulb? What if the ballast must be fixed: Is that a landlord expense? What if the light fixture burns out in the common hallway? Who tends to that? The building air-conditioning is malfunctioning. Who is responsible for fixing it? Does it matter if the HVAC unit services multiple tenants, or just one tenant? A leak occurs during a rainstorm. Is the landlord required to repair the leak? Is the landlord liable for damage to the tenant's equipment caused by the water that leaked in? Is this damage covered by insurance? If yes, does the landlord's or the tenant's policy apply? What if the leak was due to a tenant's equipment breakage on the floor above where the damage occurred? Where is the delineation of responsibility? If the lease contains a waiver of subrogation clause, how does that affect the parties and their respective insurance carriers? If the leakage was due to a malfunction in the tenant's equipment and assuming the tenant's insurance carrier covers any loss within the tenant's premises and the landlord's insurance carrier covers any loss to the common area, what if the landlord's insurance policy has a huge deductible? The damage was caused by the tenant's equipment; can the landlord at least recover the deductible from the tenant? Does the answer change if the waiver of subrogation paragraph states "Notwithstanding the foregoing provision, Tenant shall be responsible for any deductible incurred by Landlord in connection with the loss or damage?" If a guest is injured in one of the common areas such as the parking lot, is that the landlord's problem? If the injury occurs in the tenant's premises, then, is it a tenant concern? Again, is this an insurance issue? Problems of this nature are commonplace and it is management's job to address these matters.

Management concerns are varied and it is helpful to develop procedures to address at least some of the recurring issues. A few of the issues that

management must deal with include:
- Security concerns.
- Hazardous waste.
- Trash removal.
- Violations of exclusivity rights.
- Parking matters such as the need for valet parking at peak times.
- Annual testing for fire, life, and safety.
- Storage issues.
- Americans with Disabilities Act (ADA) compliance.
- Public access issues.
- Real estate taxes and related appeals.
- Emergency issues such as preparations in the event of fire and/or earthquakes.

The point is that there are many different issues and concerns that come up on a daily basis that must be addressed.

The more properties one has, the more difficult it is to keep track of the various nuisances that exist within each property. Important matters can be forgotten. By creating a booklet or binder for each property, the salient items that pertain to that property may be captured and reviewed when needed, so that decisions and finalizing documentation can be expedited.

Project Summary Binder

The Project Summary Binder for each property might contain the following:

1. Current rent roll reflecting the date prepared as well as the tenant's name, square footage, base rent, rent per square foot, commencement and expiration dates, what if any operating expenses are paid by the tenant, security deposit, options, and any special provisions such as guaranties.

2. "Cheat Sheet" summarizing what, as landlord, you are trying to achieve, as well as special or unique provisions that apply to the subject project. The Cheat Sheet should cover the type of leases in the project, that is, a triple net, modified gross, or gross lease, the scheduled rent per square foot, and the load factor.

3. Individual Lease Summaries for each lease.

4. Vacancy Chart.

5. Delinquency Report.

6. Annual Budget.

7. Leasing Flyer.

8. A narrative highlighting special lease features, such as exclusives, rights of first refusal, death and disability clauses, options to purchase and/or extend, and so forth.

9. Loan information, which should include:

  a. Loan servicer's contact information.
  - Loan number
  - Account representative's name, telephone number, email address, and mailing address.

  b. Outstanding balance.

  c. Monthly payment.

  d. Amortization.

  e. Due date.

  f. Interest rate.

  g. Right to place secondary financing.

  h. When debt is open for prepayment.

  i. Prepayment penalty/defeasance fee.

  j. Holdback provisions, if applicable.

  k. Reserves.

- Type of baskets.
- Amount held by lender per basket.
- Amount deposited per month per basket.
- Cap per basket.

l. Special features.

10. If there are percentage rent clauses in any of the leases, the breakpoint sales and the breakpoint percentage.

11. Depending on the type of project, a site plan and/or schematic plans for each floor and each suite.

12. "As-builts" for each suite and especially for any vacant space.

13. Bank account information including the depository, type of account, and balances.

14. A narrative list of specific problems that must be addressed.

15. Ownership information. If the project is syndicated, a list of the investors and their percentage ownership should be drafted.

16. How documents should be executed to bind the owner. Having a ready reference to the signature block is helpful so that every time a document is signed, there is a quick guide available.

17. A recitation of what the management fee is for the property and how it is calculated.

Assembling this type of handy reminder in a single source assists not only the property manager, but also will assist in leasing and, if kept current, as a reference guide for individuals that might be less informed than the manager about a specific property.

The Project Summary Binder should be reviewed on a monthly basis, with a focus on expiring leases, the budget (with emphasis on any income or expense line item that is outside a normal variance), delinquencies, and major and minor problems. The binder should be used as an active tool for managing the property.

Be Proactive, Not Reactive

Well-executed property management means anticipating problems and attempting to take corrective action before a major crisis arises. Being proactive can mean eschewing the path of least resistance. It is relatively easy to call the plumber when the bathroom toilet is backed up; it is a lot more difficult to ensure that the plumbing lines in a mid-rise office building have the proper slope so that potential clogs are avoided. In most areas of the country there is a rainy season. A proactive approach schedules the gutters and drains to be serviced well in advance of the rains. When it is raining and leaks are occurring due to clogged gutters, if the gutters are serviced at that point, the manager has been reactive rather than proactive. In the long run, a proactive approach is more efficient and cost-effective than a reactive approach. How many times do you want to call the roofer or the plumber, after all? Try to get a roofer out to your property when it is raining. Getting the roofer or a handyman to check out potential problems before they become a problem is usually a wiser approach and less costly in the long run.

There is no easy way to avoid problems, which usually are property specific. The key is to take the time to view the subject property from top to bottom, identifying potential areas of concern: Is there any area where the grade of the floor is so steep so that a trip hazard may arise? Do the elevators have a motion sensor to avoid closing prematurely? Is the surface of the lobby too slick, which may lead to someone falling down? Is the external lighting adequate for visitors? Have reasonable security measures been taken to prevent theft? Are the trees routinely trimmed so as to avoid damage to parked cars in the event of a severe storm? The list, of course, goes on. A proactive approach attempts to anticipate and address potential concerns well in advance of the problem occurring.

Monitoring

Monitoring is a review process to oversee that employees are properly carrying out their assigned tasks and also making sure tenants are honoring their lease obligations.

Monitoring employee performance should not necessarily have a negative connotation. The objective is to be encouraging and render constructive, positive feedback. For example, let us say the onsite manager is attempting to lease a vacant space in the Center. A discussion with the manager might reveal that he has not approached the other tenants in the Center with an incentive program to encourage them to bring potential tenant leads to the manager. Now the situation can be swiftly corrected, to the mutual benefit of all.

Mundane matters must also be monitored. Is every lease being abstracted? Are the leases being scanned? Are errors being made in imputing the lease data into the computer?

The project delinquency report should be reviewed monthly. Are the tenants paying their rent in a timely manner? If there are significant delinquencies, a discussion should be had with the property manager to determine a proper course of action. Is the delinquency an ongoing problem, or a rough spot for a tenant who is making a sincere effort to honor his obligations? Is a rent deferment program appropriate, or should a three-day notice to pay or quit be issued? These issues are crucial to the economic viability of the project and therefore should be monitored closely.

At times there are also nonmonetary lease obligations that must be consistently reviewed. An example of this type of obligation is the tenant's obligation to maintain insurance. The landlord wants to make sure that the tenant carries the required insurance to protect against loss within the premises as well as the economic viability of that tenant in the event of a casualty. For example, if a fire occurs at the center, the landlord's obligation to carry fire insurance ensures that the structures will be rebuilt, and the loss of rents provision pays the tenant's rent during the 12-or 18-month period covered by the policy. What if the tenant fails to maintain adequate contents coverage? Its loss in terms of damaged goods and equipment might be so substantial that the tenant cannot afford to reopen.

In conjunction with shopping centers, the tenant's sales volume is often a good barometer of the financial health of that tenant. Tenants required to pay percentage rent must disclose sales results. Also, large tenants, such as the anchor, are often required to supply this information. In contrast, for small or medium-sized centers retail sales, volumes are normally not readily forwarded to the landlord.

If a store's sales volume is obtained, translating that dollar figure into monthly and annual sales per square foot is very helpful for evaluating performance. Different industries have different profit margins, but usually industry statistics will show what price per square foot represents breakeven and what are, in general, the reasonable sales per square foot needed to have a successful business.

Reporting

Everyone reports to someone. Day porters report to managers. Managers report to owners. Owners report to investors and lenders. Lenders report to shareholders, and so on.

If the project is syndicated and there are third-party investors, it is important to keep them advised as to the status of the project. A status report should, at a minimum, go out yearly, and preferably at least quarterly. The report should comment on the overall health of the project: occupancy levels, cash flow, and cash reserves. Also, new developments, such as leasing that has been recently entered into, should be mentioned. Lastly, problem areas and major issues, such as how a maturing loan is being dealt with, should be covered.

With the advent of the computer and especially the Internet, consideration should be given to posting project financial results, that is, rent roll, balance sheet, and income and expense numbers, on a monthly basis. Investors could access this information on the Web through the use of a password so that the financial data remains confidential.

Management as a Business

Viewing one property, the fee for managing the asset is fairly simple. The fee is usually a percentage of the gross income collected: typically 3 to 5 percent. The management may be internal or conducted by an outside management firm. If it is done internally, there is usually not an exact identity of interest between the property ownership and management. A typical ownership structure might involve investors that are passive, not involved in the day-to-day affairs of the property. The equation becomes more complicated when multiple properties are owned and the same key entrepreneurs are involved as partners and as the owners of the management entity.

The management fee should be monitored and reviewed on an annual basis. Given the inherent conflict of interest between the managers and the owners, any modification of the management fee should be approved by the partnership.

In the beginning of this chapter, I mention that each property should be viewed as a stand-alone asset, a separate profit center. The same holds true for the management income. The analysis becomes much more complicated when multiple properties are involved and overhead is incurred, including salaries and office expenses to run the property management business. A distinction must be made between a property expense and an expense attributable to the management company. Should any or all of the property manager's income be borne by the asset, or is it 100 percent attributable to the operating company? The profitability of the management company must be monitored and controlled as a stand-alone business similar to each individual property.

Conclusion

> ### Rule Number 31
> Marketing, leasing, and management are interconnected and interdependent. Care should be taken to integrate all three of these areas cohesively.

The next chapter discusses the area about how to structure your venture. You are in the process of acquiring a real estate investment. You have analyzed it thoroughly, you have gone through the leases and composed a detailed income and expense analysis, and you have arranged appropriate financing and considered the tax implications. You have also put on paper a marketing game plan. Your leasing and management team is in place, but how do you structure the acquisition in terms of your relationship with your potential partners? The next chapter addresses this issue.

www.ingramcontent.com/pod-product-compliance
Lightning Source LLC
Chambersburg PA
CBHW082250220526
45469CB00009B/2940